STEVE YOUNG
Staying in the Pocket

STEVE YOUNG
Staying in the Pocket

Dick Harmon

Black Moon Publishing, L.L.C.
Salt Lake City, Utah

Library of Congress Catalog Card Number: 95-71466

ISBN 1-887955-99-2

1st Printing, 1995

Printed in the United States of America

To AnnaLee

Contents

Picture Credits

FOREWORD

Getting Steve Young to participate in writing a book is somewhat like getting the star quarterback to stay in the pocket and get mowed over by a pass rusher. It is not in his nature. There are numerous authors and publishers who will attest to this fact. Over the years, many have approached, proposed, and outlined possible projects for him to throw himself into. This work is no exception, I tried and failed to tackle Steve Young with a book. But in researching this book I learned a lesson from the subject: Don't get discouraged if what you truly believe in encounters some tough obstacles. Just do it.

Some day there will be a book written on or by Steve Young that has Young explaining his life in his own voice. It probably will be a book about principles, geared for youth. But at the present time, that literary work is not a reality. Steve Young is a very self-effacing person. He goes out of his way to make his importance, his accomplishments, and his virtues appear as nothing. If you know Steve Young, you will take note that he is not a self-promoter and does not blow his own horn. He dresses as if he would like to be average, drab, almost a slob. Until recently he drove an old junker with 260,000 miles on it.

When Steve became a professional athlete and received a million dollar signing bonus, he kept the check wadded up in his pants' pocket for days. The check represented a major change in his status in life that he wasn't quite sure about.

A book extolling stories about Steve Young goes against his nature. Perhaps that is why, during a dizzy off-season following his first Super Bowl victory, Young has had little time or interest in book proposals. I didn't take his reticence to be involved in this project personally, I just made it a personal challenge to create and finish a project whose time is ripe. So Young is off the hook. He had nothing to do with the creation of this book and, if questioned, cornered, or criticized for its contents, he can truthfully deny any direct participation.

The format for this book changed three or four times before publication. One constant from the beginning was that it would be written in the third person. In other words, this was never intended to be an "I did this" or "I did that" manuscript. Quotes attributed to Steve Young have been taken from public and private interviews published in general-circulation magazines, newspapers, public appearances, press conferences, and the recollections of friends. The strength of the book is in the witness of other people, offering their opinions and views on Steve Young.

An example of the power of these witnesses is a story told by Kay Warner, development director for the "I Can Read Program," which named Steve Young as its honorary chairman. Young's Forever Young Foundation provides financial support for the program which helps elementary school children learn to read. Warner asked Young to make an appearance at a shopping Mall in Salt Lake City, where more than 250 children in the program had gathered.

Young had a very busy schedule and had some apprehension about fitting the appearance into his calendar, but he came. The busloads of children pulled up to the mall and Young positioned himself to hand out 250 autographed footballs. Most of the children had composed essays which they brought with them. Warner saw a transformation take place in both Young and the children. "When Steve sat down, he started reading these essays and commenting to each child about what they had written. Needless to say the kids were excited. But the thing I noticed most was how genuine Steve was with those kids, and they knew it. We had one sixth-grade boy, who had showed little interest in reading, come away that day with a complete attitude change. His teachers have commented what an impact that had. What had an impact on me was how much time and interest Steve Young put into this once he got there. It was dramatic."

Steve Young would never sit down with a reporter and tell a story about himself the way Warner did. This is what this book is about, relating and recounting key elements that help comprise the person who is professional football's Most Valuable Player.

This book would not have been printed if it were not for consistent prodding, challenging, and urging from a handful of friends and family members who believed it should be written. My brother Kent, son Brandon, and wife AnnaLee were relentless in their efforts to see the pages of this book in print. Many days and late nights they were the main motivation for working on this project.

My neighbor and friend Bruce Bushnell, a Steve Young fanatic, also impressed me with his faith that a work about this unique NFL star was needed.

I must thank two writers and interviewers who helped me meet some very close deadlines. Charlene Winters and Doug Fox came to the plate and registered some hits at crucial times. Other members of the Fourth Estate who collected many quotes during post-game press conferences helped piece together parts of stories whose significance over time have proved important to the Young saga. I make no pretense here to have been present at the many games and practices over the years where these stories of Young developed.

In researching these stories, I recognize the work of writers at *Sports Illustrated, Sport Magazine*, the *San Francisco Chronicle, San Jose Mercury News, Deseret News, Daily Herald, Salt Lake Tribune,* and *Miami Herald*. All of these newspapers and magazines have swapped Young tales over the years, often utilizing dispatches from the Associated Press and other wire services.

The Young story is continuing to be written chapter by chapter. This is an attempt to tell the tale up to the present time of a remarkable athlete. Young is not the type of person who toots his own horn. We have taken the trumpet in hand for him in the pages of this book. His is a horn worth blowing.

"The narrower the cage, the sweeter the Liberty."—German Proverb

POCKET SENSE, POCKET CHANGE

Einstein, the father of the atomic age, had trouble passing a math class. Beethoven slowly became deaf but still was able to compose timeless masterpieces. Stevie Wonder can't see yet paints remarkable musical pictures. And Steve Young, the highest-rated National Football League (NFL) passer in history, has had trouble staying in the pocket.

The "pocket" is a protected work area created five to eight yards behind the line of scrimmage by five or six body-sacrificing linemen. A pass-protection pocket lasts for only a few precious seconds, just long enough for the quarterback to find an open receiver or get smothered by oncoming defensive linemen. A scrambling quarterback who prematurely leaves the pocket will occasionally turn in one or two big plays, but, most often will lose yardage and short-circuit the productivity of designed plays. To become a championship quarterback in the NFL one must control that self preserving urge to run and master the art of staying in the pocket.

A scrambling Steve Young calmly evades
Washington Redskin defensive tackle Bobby Wilson.

Steve Young, considered sort of a stiff and straight-arrow by many, appears to have always done the noble thing socially, sticking to the conservative confines of the "pocket" that nests his traditional "Mormon" values. He has shown that he can stand patiently against an extraordinary rush of opposition to complete his life's goals. However, when it comes to football, his happy, anxious feet have found multiple ways of slipping out of the pocket and getting in and out of trouble. While Young's feet have many times carried him to big plays and chunks of yardage, his lightning-quick speed has also stood in the way of him becoming a complete quarterback throughout most of his football career.

But lately, something has come over Young: the league's Most Valuable Player has painstakingly controlled his urges to run with the football except on rare occasions. Characterized as one of the most dangerous and able scramblers in the NFL, Young is finally mastering the art of setting up behind his blockers, surveying the field, and waiting for a play to develop as targets clear of defensive players. He then fires darts on time with General Patton-type authority and laser-guided accuracy. As a result, he is taking his game to a level few quarterbacks have attained. Such control in a pass-protection pocket has been every quarterback's goal; for Young, just getting there has been a lifelong challenge.

Young's mastery of the art of quarterbacking is tracked by looking at the average times per game he has tried running the football since getting significant playing time with the San Francisco 49ers. During the 1991-92 season Young averaged 6.7 attempts at running the football per game. The next season, 1992-93, that dropped to 4.7 attempts per game. In 1993-94 Young left the pocket to run an average of 4.3 times per game.

Then in 1994-95, the fleet-footed quarterback averaged just 3.6 rushes per game. Young was finally trusting the wisdom of staying in the pocket.

In 1994 Young's newly acquired pocket proficiency earned him and his Niner teammates Super Bowl rings. Young's 112.8 pass-efficiency rating was the best ever recorded for a NFL quarterback.

Staying in the pocket not only took on a new meaning for Young and the 49er offense but for opposing teams as well. You see, if you take the quarterback and leave him in the pocket, a defense can design schemes which concentrate on breaking down the effectiveness of the pass play. Defensive linemen can lay back their ears and charge the passer. Linebackers can cross-step like ballerinas chasing backs and tight ends, or they can drop into zone coverage. The secondary can focus strictly on coverage. As long as the quarterback is confined to the pocket, there can be some order to the organized fight we call football.

But when the quarterback leaves the pocket, not recklessly, not in panic or indecision, but in a precise and timed maneuver, in the case of Steve Young, all hell breaks loose.

Just ask the 49ers' long-toothed National Football Conference enemies, the Dallas Cowboys, recent two-time world champions and owners of the NFL's top ranked defense in 1994. The Dallas Cowboys, generally considered to be the major roadblock for the San Francisco 49ers' Super Bowl dreams, played the 49ers twice in the 1994 season. Both times, contrary to the confrontations of the past, Young stayed in the pocket, launching arrows like Robin Hood on steroids. But Young also did the unthinkable in his new style. Young vacated the pocket at opportune times—controlled and planned times—and caught the reigning champs completely off guard.

November 13, 1994 in Candlestick Park marked the tenth game of the season for San Francisco. On deck, Barry Switzer's Cowboys, sporting a lofty 8–1 record. The 49ers were 7–2 and had thirsted all season for this rematch with their longtime NFC rivals. The number one ranked defense in football versus the precise 49er offense. For most of the game Young stayed within the confines of the pocket and slowly picked apart the Dallas secondary. But there was a time in this 21–14 win when Young, targeted for Cowboy punishment in the pocket, turned to his old ways, scrambled outside the pocket and humbled the Dallas mighty front seven.

The Cowboy defense was ready for the new Young, constantly pressuring Young as he dropped back to pass. Time and time again, Dallas defenders pressured the 49er quarterback into getting rid of the ball early, sacking him twice and knocking him down after half a dozen pass plays. Then it happened. The play came down from the press box for Young to leave the pocket. Young dropped back, faked a handoff to running back Ricky Watters, then, pivoting around to his left, triggered a perfectly executed bootleg run, sprinting around the pass rush, curling around the end and heading into the secondary free as a cat in a huge canary cage.

The 49er call was bold, brave, and unpredictable. Young, the league's highest-paid player at the time, was running the football like a halfback. But the play wasn't born of panic or a rushed decision. This play was by design.

Switzer, the Dallas coach, was stunned. The 49ers had called Young's number and stripped him of the protection of any blockers as the flow of the play went the other direction. It was crazy. But it worked. The move unraveled the Cowboy defense. Young picked up 25 yards on the play. Shaking his head before reporters afterwards, Switzer mused, "They were willing to sacrifice Young. We were kind of surprised." Young went

Steve Young - Staying in the Pocket.

on to run for sixty yards, throw for two touchdowns and score on a quarterback sneak the third Niner touchdown. Expecting Young to stay in the pocket, had caught Dallas with their cleats untied.

Two weeks before Super Bowl XXIX came the rematch between Dallas and San Francisco in the NFC championship game. A year earlier, the Cowboys had whipped the 49ers and revenge played a giant factor in San Francisco's preparation for a second showdown. During the week, Cowboy players said Young wouldn't snooker them again. If Young ran on them again, he'd be finger food. Trash talk reigned on the airwaves and in the headlines all week long. A fight broke out before kickoff at Candlestick Park between the two teams. Emotions ran at high tide.

But Young's effectiveness in the previous showdown had taken something out of the Cowboys. Dallas' proud and cocky defense never sacked Young the entire game. Young threw for 155 yards on 13 of 29 attempts with two of the passes going for touchdowns. And at key times he did leave the pocket, once for a touchdown.

The 49ers were Super Bowl bound to face the San Diego Chargers. All that remained was taking orders for ring sizes. Wrote USA Today's Larry Weisman of Super Bowl day: "Young, using the pass as a straight razor, nicked and sliced the Chargers until they hung in bloody ribbons."

The Steve Young saga has been a tale of ups and downs, disappointments and triumphs. His conflicts have been real live ghosts and inner demons that have tested the life pocket that surrounds him. But he has patiently stayed in that pocket with a style and grace that continues to amaze all who know him.

In these crazy times in professional sports it is nearly impossible for a superstar to survive the madness of big money and fame without revealing chinks in his armor. But Young has managed to become a superstar while maintaining a life-style worthy of emulation.

"Steve Young is a guy you'd want your daughter to marry," crowed San Francisco 49er owner Eddie DeBartolo, Jr. Young has the money, the smarts, the looks, and the job. But those who know him realize the star is much more than he appears.

Even though Steve Young has now been on the cover of *GQ,* 49er return specialist Dexter Carter has said of Young's dressing habits, "Steve doesn't seem to know that certain things go together and certain things don't. I've seen him mismatch all six important parts of an ensemble—socks, shoes, pants, belt, shirt and jacket. I tell you what, though, the way he plays on Sundays, in a uniform, looks beautiful."

Someone once said fashion is the art of seeming rather than being. *People Magazine* named Young one of the fifty most beautiful people in the world. Young has fought perceptions about himself all his life, and the magazine complement just goes in the file. "The reality is, I know different," he remarked.

Young knows there are also perceptions about the pocket—about just being there and doing something when you are in there. "The response on a football field is that you can hide and not give your best effort because with all those bodies flying around, nobody will notice. The reality is you have to give your best effort all the time so your team-mates will believe in you. Sometimes towards the end of a game when you are losing there is a feeling that you can slack off because this one is gone and we can get after it next week. The reality is championships are not won next week, they are won today. You don't compete against other people, you compete against yourself."

"No success can compensate for failure in the home." —David O. McKay

POCKET ROOTS

Actor Danny Glover said his greatest heroes in life were his mother and father. Parents do have a way of impacting children in ways that continue to astound social scientists.

LeGrande and Sherry Young are parents whose inner compasses have been stuck on a very lucky path, a road some may call the right trail. Their oldest child, Jon Steven Young, is recognized as the top quarterback in the NFL. He is also one of the league's highest-paid players. He exudes success and is a charismatic role model. Their second son, Mike, is married with three children and will soon finish a three-year residency as a physician in Grand Rapids, Michigan. Tom, the third son, also married, is bound for medical school after finishing his college eligibility as a quarterback at Brigham Young University and playing professional football on a team in Finland. Daughter Melissa, also married, is a public-relations spokesman for NuSkin International in Provo, Utah. Jim, the couple's fourth son, is the lone sibling at home, drudging through the teenage years, and doing it by the numbers.

The Youngs may be too modest to admit it, but they could have written the script on how to raise kids. Of course, they are not perfect. Their kids are courteous, hard-working, kind, sensitive, responsible, tactful, dependable, charitable, honorable, and even humble. They are so good, you almost want to slap them just to see what they'd do.

LeGrande Young is the patriarch, a staunch teacher and leader who is as much a disciplinarian as he is a philosopher. When he was six years old he earned the nickname "Grit," and, according to Steve, people better call him Grit because he doesn't like being called LeGrande.

Sherry is the loving, kind, beautiful mother who has been at the side of each child, cheering their successes and, when needed, wiping away their tears.

"When Mr. Young told you to do something," neighbor Frank Arnone told Joan Ryan of the *San Jose Mercury News*, "you didn't question it."

Grit and Sherry's story began in the 1950s, a time when America looked at "Leave it to Beaver" on TV and wondered if their family was like that of the Beav and Wally. Sherry Steed met Grit Young at the home of Joan Peterson, now Joan Fisher, of Salt Lake City. Grit had just settled into college life at Brigham Young University in his home town of Provo, Utah.

Sherry immediately liked Grit because he had just returned from Australia, sacrificing two years of his life for religious service, and he was a football player. Both were devout Mormons, members of the Church of Jesus Christ of Latter-day Saints. Grit's missionary service was a big deal in his life and Sherry wanted to marry a man who had served such a mission. Sherry was upbeat, positive, vivacious—the kind of woman who can light up a room when she enters. Both joined social clubs at school and immediately had an active calendar for dating. Grit was looking to marry right away; but a year went by

10

LeGrand "Grit" Young at BYU.

and the two had dated and broken up several times before they actually tied the knot.

Grit was a very hard-working student. On the football field he set a single season BYU rushing record for the Cougars in the late 1950s, although one of his coaches remembers him as a very slow-footed running back. He studied hard. He attacked problems in his calculus class relentlessly, never putting the work aside until he had figured it out. He was a problem solver all the way, remembers Joan Fisher. "He always stuck with something and got things done." This trait was particularly attractive to Sherry.

Grit viewed the role of a man and woman in a very traditional sense. It was his responsibility as the husband and father to work and provide for his family; it was Sherry's job to take care of the home and be the primary nurturing agent for the children. Luckily for Grit he married a woman who not only fit that role but welcomed the challenge. When Sherry gave birth to the only daughter in the family, Melissa, Grit expressed anxiety: "What do I know about raising a girl?" But he did just fine.

Grit Young is a staunch believer in discipline and obedience, and he expected nothing less from his children. As toddlers, they were expected to obey their parents and toe the line. Grit had a reputation as a rough-and-tough guy, taking on the football image. But Sherry saw a deeply religious person whose values were solidly grounded in their faith. Grit asked a lot of his children; they may not have liked it all the time, but they generally followed the well-established rules in the Young household. There was little deviation from his direction.

"People always say Steve got his toughness from his dad, but I believe he got his toughness from his mother. Sherry is a very strong person. She works extremely hard in keeping the family together, on track and headed in the right direction.

Sherry Young is one of the most ardent protective mothers you will ever meet," claims Joan Fisher. "She has stood up for her children before neighbors and even Grit. She is fearless when it comes to standing up for her family."

Another Grit and Sherry Young trait is family priority. Says Fisher, "With these two, their family always came first and foremost in their schedules and lives. I've kept in touch with Sherry and Grit the past 40 years and when I go back to New York to see Sherry and we plan to go out together, Sherry refuses to alter the part of her schedule that includes a 5 a.m. wakeup call to run Jimmy to a church seminary. She wouldn't change it, get somebody else to do it, or just write it off that day—it was something she did every day and she did it that day before we got together."

"Sherry is not a person who gets her feelings hurt easily. She can take a lot from people and she has a very positive nature about her," says Fisher. "This is also a family who has never been into money. They have never been caught up in having things like gorgeous furniture and clothes. It just never mattered to them and was not a priority."

Grit was raised in a modest home in Provo. He worked all his life doing what he could to earn a few extra dollars. He picked cherries, worked on a sheep ranch, fought forest fires, dug ditches and paths, and worked a chain saw. During a fire watch he could work 72 hours straight without sleep.

Grit traces his roots back to Mormon Pioneer leader Brigham Young. The exact genealogy goes along these lines: Brigham Young married Emily Dow Partridge. One of their daughters was Emily Augusta Young, who married Hyrum Bradley Clawson. They had Carlie Louine Clawson, who married Seymour Bicknell Young. They had Scott Richmond Young, who married Louise Leonard; and they had LeGrande Young, who married Sherry Steed. They had Jon Steven Young.

Steve was born October 11, 1961, in Salt Lake City, Utah. The family moved to Greenwich, Connecticut when he was six years old. There Grit took a job as a corporate attorney in nearby Manhattan. He later secured a job in Greenwich and cut out the commute to New York City. Greenwich is a posh enclave outside of New York City and is home to Barbara Streisand, Frank and Kathy Lee Gifford, and corporate headquarters for Xerox corporation. The home Grit Young bought in Greenwich for $75,000 a quarter of a century ago is still the family's headquarters. The modest two-story home located off Split Timber Road is miles from the huge mansions that dot parts of Greenwich.

A few of Grit's rules for his kids included instruction to abstain from smoking and drinking, while also avoiding caffeine in coffee or soft drinks. "Growing up in Connecticut, I used to think there were only four Mormons in the world—me, my parents and Brigham Young. But my friends always respected it," said Steve. "I was always the guy who drove everyone else home. When we went out at night, my friends would buy their beer and they'd buy me a gallon of milk." Young refused to drink alcohol, but nobody begrudged him his milk.

The Young family bounced around a few principles which are a little different from those of some of the so-called nuclear families of today. First and foremost, Grit and Sherry Young have kept their love for each other alive and watched it mature along with their children. Although Greenwich, even in the late 1960s, was full of the rich and famous, the Youngs kept their lives simple.

Grit demanded his children do their part, whether it was family chores, outside jobs, or playing on a team. "Dad always demanded that we work hard," says Tom. Grit bought his family cars from his employer and worked on them himself, teaching his children in the process. The Young children had a newspaper route which was passed down from Steve to Mike, then to Tommy, Melissa, and Jimmy.

Even after Steve Young became, for a time, the NFL's highest-paid player and helped his parents, brothers, and sister financially, Sherry Young still works as a substitute teacher at both the junior and senior high school level.

"A principle," Steve explains, "is a basic truth, law or assumption. The definition also includes moral, ethical standards along with a basic or essential quality. Principles then, should be timeless. We should feel confident and secure in the fact that while circumstances may change, the very world may change, but true principles will stand no matter what new challenges may arise."

Grit was always there to back his children, but he did not interfere, especially when it came to sports and teams. Says Tom, "He would stay out of the politics of the teams we were on. He supported us but never stuck his nose in things like some fathers do." That gave the children a sense of responsibility. He may have fixed cars, but some things in life he wanted his children to learn how to fix.

"He was always big on relationships," said Steve after he was voted by 49er teammates in 1992 as the recipient of the Eshmont Award, given annually to the player who showed the most leadership and inspiration. "He always told me, 'If you don't want to be part of the team, then go play golf or tennis.' He was big on playing your part. He made me stick with things. He was the kind of guy that when I'd wake up Saturday mornings, say 9 a.m., which is pretty early for a teenager, and I was supposed to, you know, mow the lawn, well the lawn mower would be going. He would want me to come sprinting out so he could say, 'I couldn't wait all day.' The old 'I delivered papers in the snow' business. He wanted you to do everything perfect. And to keep you humble."

15

Steve remembers himself as a shy, scared boy who refused to go to the second grade without his mother. When growing up he used to think of excuses why he couldn't go on an overnight Boy Scouts camping trip, because he was afraid to leave home. "I could lie to you and say I was macho, but I wasn't. The most traumatic experience of my life was getting on the airplane and going to college at BYU."

Steve used to sit in the back of the classroom, hoping nobody would notice him. He used to wear a ski cap to make his hair straight because he thought people with curly hair were weird. "I look back at my life and I am amazed that I've been able to accomplish some of the things I have done so far. I was challenged to do something that for me was humanly impossible to do."

But today Steve has apparently survived. He had the fortune of being raised by Grit and Sherry, a set of parents who believed in themselves as much as they did in him. The Young household was quite a secure pocket to call home. For Steve Young it always has been the ultimate pocket.

"Only dead fish swim with the stream." — Unknown

MAKING THE GRADE

Grit Young never pushed any of his sons into competing in sports. Grit's philosophy was that if the boys wanted to play they should go after it; he would support them. He attended as many games as his work schedule made possible. Sherry Young rarely missed a game.

The one time Grit did coach Steve in Little League, the boy asked his father not to take the job again. Steve was afraid people would think he got his playing time or position because his father was the coach. To Steve this was definitely unacceptable.

In this setting Steve Young grew up a competitive young boy. He tried to win at everything he did—from tiddly-winks to baseball and football. The usual victim of his competition was brother Mike, just two years younger. The two would tangle in the yard and Steve wouldn't quit at any game until he won. Mike was a lean, tall boy. Steve was stockier, stronger, more muscular. He was also gifted with very quick reflexes and footspeed that was the fastest around town.

Steve was always a person with tremendous drive and motivation. Whether it be collecting stamps or baseball cards, playing catch or doing school work, he worked extremely hard

Steve Young and his taller younger brother, Mike.

at excelling at the task. "He was the most driven of all the children," says his third-grade teacher Lee Spong. "He was the kind of kid who was so special that he stays in your heart."

Steve seemed to care about everything—winning and looking good in the process were both priorities. He was not only a naturally gifted athlete, blessed with timing, balance and strength, he liked to perfect his talents. He practiced and worked to get better. Steve Young's hero was Dallas Cowboy quarterback Roger Staubach, a charismatic leader and clutch performer. During that era, Staubach and Terry Bradshaw were the best quarterbacks in the NFL. Steve dreamed of playing in the NFL but little did he imagine in his wildest dreams that he would someday outperform both of Staubach and Bradshaw, and do it after a very trying experience of playing second fiddle to one of the greatest quarterbacks who ever played the game—Joe Montana. And then he would post numbers that would supersede even those of Montana.

Younger brother Mike, who followed him by just two years, had trouble keeping up with Steve's deeds and accomplishments. "Steve was a very uptight person to be around. Everything mattered." Steve was a straight-A student in high school and became a member of the National Honor Society. Because his curriculum included some college courses and he had a perfect 4.0 grade-point average on the regular courses, he earned a 4.2 GPA, superseding the standard mark of excellence. Steve Young was not a rocket-scientist or brain-surgeon type of student; but he was smart enough to know how to study and figure out the game plan in the classroom, and then go out and perform when assignments and tests were given.

In keeping with Grit's edict that his children work for their spending money, Steve took up mowing lawns in Greenwich, handling a newspaper route, and working part-time at

Carvel's Ice Cream Shop. Subsequently, because of his drive and abilities, other kids flocked to him. He was voted team captain of the baseball, basketball, and football teams at Greenwich High School. Whenever a group of his peers would get together for some common purpose in school, church, or just as friends, Steve naturally floated to the surface as the leader. He spoke French fluently and took advanced calculus classes in high school.

Once during the Greenwich High basketball season, the center on the team was playing poorly. The coach, Garland Allen, decided he had to do something about it and pondered what he would say in the locker room at halftime. Allen pushed open the locker room door and there stood Steve Young delivering to his teammate the exact type of speech the coach had planned to deliver himself. Allen had nothing else to say and asked the team to get back out and play.

When the Greenwich Cardinal football team added New Yorker Ron Saggese as an assistant coach during Steve Young's senior year, the new coach phoned back to his city buddies and said of Steve: "If I were to tell you the story of this kid, it would make you puke." Young, to Saggese's surprise, did not drink, smoke, or swear. He pitched a no-hitter the day after the senior prom because he was the only player who was not hung-over from partying the night before.

Near his Greenwich home there was a route Steve used to run to help keep himself in shape during high school. The route had two directions that led to a loop for a good workout. If he went one way, he would take a short cut. The other way was longer. The fork in the route was 400 yards from his driveway and when he'd go out for a run, he'd have to make up his mind which way he'd go. He recalled: "That wasn't always easy. It was tempting to take the shortcut instead of the longer way and it was a challenge to take the long route. But I knew if I

20

went the long way I'd be better off and I'd be in better shape. I convinced myself to go the longer way by telling myself if I took the shortcut, something bad would happen; I would break my leg or my foot or something."

In reality, Young was just following his bloodlines. Grit knew few shortcuts. Steve did not know how to cheat himself either.

Greenwich high school football coach Mike Ornato used an option-attack offense with the Cardinals, and passing the ball was a rare event—one of the last things a quarterback would do. Steve Young, who was already turning the heads of college scouts with his speed, rarely threw the football. "Hey, if I threw the football in high school, it wasn't in public. I threw a lot of things when I was growing up, like tantrums and stuff like that, but rarely did I throw a football." Steve disdained passing the football. It may have had something to do with one junior varsity game in which he threw eight interceptions in a rainstorm with a wet ball.

The group of athletes who played with Steve Young were not heralded in the beginning. His sophomore year people labeled that class the "Lousy Bunch." After watching one of the disappointing junior varsity games with the "Lousy Bunch" Ornato told his staff he needed to have a talk with the group. "It was a real serious talk," said Ornato. "They had embarrassed themselves on the field, and I told them they had two miserable years ahead of them if they didn't think about it and get it together."

A challenge like that was decisive for Steve Young. If somebody threw down the gauntlet, he would be first in line to say, "bring it on." Young began a pattern right then which he would continue: if there was a challenge, he would always be one to run to the end of the board and take the plunge. The key word here is RUN.

21

Steve Young earned the starting quarterback job during his junior year when Bill Barber, the starting senior, injured his shoulder. Ornato put in Young during a practice scrimmage against New Canaan High. On the first offensive play by the Cardinals, Young dropped back to pass and promptly dropped the football on the grass. But then an amazing thing happened. Young picked the football off the turf, surveyed the oncoming tacklers and took off. Moments later he had zigzagged through defenders and scored a touchdown on a 70-yard run.

Ornato had a quarterback. He also had a star.

During their senior year, the "Lousy Bunch" won the west division title and played in the Connecticut state championship game. By that time, Steve Young, a lightning-quick runner who could cut on a dime and explode down the field, had earned the nickname "The Magician." During this time in his athletic career, Steve confidently relied on his legs. Whenever he was in trouble in the pocket or while holding the football waiting for blockers to develop a play, he was very good at just tearing away and running with the ball. Few opponents could keep up with him. His acceleration was as good as anybody's on the field. He could change directions, fake out tacklers, and sprint out of their reach very easily. That ability became a weapon Young has fine-tuned throughout his college and NFL careers. It has always been his ace in the hole and yet his greatest obstacle to becoming a complete quarterback.

His senior year at Greenwich, Steve Young ran the ball 165 times for more than 1,900 yards. But it was the whole package that impressed people at Greenwich High. Steve refused to be ordinary. Terrence Lowe, who has taught at Greenwich High since 1966, remembers one time Steve Young received a C grade in advance-placement calculus. "It was one of the few he ever had, but it didn't matter. It was an intellectual challenge for him and he refused to give in, he made up his mind to fight it, and he did," recalled Lowe. "What you see now is the real Steve Young and it has always been the real Steve Young." Lowe, who coaches swimming and water polo, labels Young as a rare student athlete. "One of the things I remember about him was how bright he was, how enthusiastic he was and how disciplined he was with a task at hand. He has always been delightful; always positive, always optimistic. He's the kind of guy who would always run to center field and then run back in. The characteristics you see were there in high school."

"Both of us," Lowe told the *San Jose Mercury News*, "were heavily involved in athletic and intellectual pursuits, so we'd talk all the time about challenging yourself intellectually and athletically and how you get a balance in your life. I knew I was an influence on him and we shared a lot of ideas, but I didn't know how much he thought of me. It just happened when he needed help, I was there, and I was someone he trusted. I tell you what, I'm happy as hell for him It couldn't happened to a nicer guy. He has a wonderful mind, and there's a feeling at the high school that his going to BYU and completing his law degree is as much an achievement as is making it in pro football. A lesser person would have broken under the pressure of the ups and downs he's going through. I've always thought he was a class act."

In his high school yearbook Steve Young wrote: "To dream and strive for those dreams. To enjoy victory and grow stronger with defeat. To live life to the fullest and fill other lives with joy. That is success."

*"Sparrows who emulate peacocks are
likely to break a thigh." — Burmese
proverb*

FIGHT OR QUIT?

Few people understand the situation Steve Young stepped into when he chose to play college football at Brigham Young University. The school may have been named after his famous pioneer ancestor, but that didn't give him any pull. Although Steve Young had some quarterbacking skills, he was about to take a giant step in his life, and everything pointed to an uphill battle all the way.

Under head coach LaVell Edwards, the BYU football program had exploded into an aerial circus, churning out All-American quarterbacks with eye-popping passing statistics. In a sense, Edwards had created a monster. Every time he launched a great quarterback, there was pressure to follow up with another. When Gary Shiede left, Gifford Nielsen picked up the pigskin and began throwing it. When Gifford Nielsen went on to play for the Houston Oilers, Marc Wilson took up the attack on the NCAA record book.

Wilson earned All-America honors in 1979 and then left for the Oakland Raiders. The Cougar passing attack remained as healthy as ever with a young brash quarterback named

Steve Young surviving college life at BYU.

Jim McMahon. Behind McMahon were no less than seven aspiring quarterbacks. One of them was a homesick freshman recruit named Steve Young.

Although he was a Mormon, it was not automatic that Steve Young would end up at the Mormon school located in Provo, Utah. As an option quarterback he had turned the heads of many Ivy League schools his senior year at Greenwich. He also got a good look from Army. But the school that showed the most interest was the University of North Carolina. Coach Dick Crum wanted the fleet-footed Young as his quarterback of the future. Crum put on a heavy rush, visiting the Young household in Greenwich and inviting Steve to Chapel Hill for a visit. If Young had correctly read all the signals he was getting from BYU recruiters, he should have ended up at North Carolina, tossing the pitch-out option and running the football.

BYU early on showed only marginal interest in Young. All Steve's friends who had attended BYU came back excited about what they'd found. And his father had played football at BYU. His parents had met each other there. The school held a strong appeal; but interest from the football program there was nothing compared to that of Crum at North Carolina.

In nearby Scarsdale, New York, a Mormon ecclesiastical leader named Ted Simmons called BYU's football office to lobby for Steve. So too did Steve's uncle Bob Steed, who lived in Utah. Steed sent the coaches a bunch of press clippings. The two men made their pitches for Steve long and hard, but it was not until December 1979 that BYU really responded. By then Young's senior year of high school football was behind him. BYU invited him to Provo for an official recruiting visit.

During the three-day visit, LaVell Edwards told Young he wasn't sure he had a scholarship for him. Before Young left for home, Edwards did report to the athlete that he had found a scholarship for him but it was not clear how Steve would fit into the program. If Edwards had only known then what he knew today, he would have had the Mormon Tabernacle Choir and a red carpet out for Steve Young.

Steve Young thus picked his school more than it picked him. His first months away from home were miserable. Always a homebody, Steve got homesick easily. He hated being away from his family and familiar surroundings. The first semester in Provo he refused to unpack his bags and called home almost every night. With seven other quarterbacks ahead of him, Steve believed going into spring football practice that he was doomed to be forgotten. It looked hopeless. Heartsick for home, one night he called home and told Grit he'd had it, he wanted to quit. Grit then gave him some advice which has stuck with Steve the rest of his life. "You can quit if you want to. But you can't come home. This is not a place for a quitter."

Steve decided to stay, gut it out, and compete. Although still homesick, he buckled down for the long haul.

Unfortunately, this despairing, discouraging and depressing type of situation would be repeated over and over again in the coming years for Steve. This first cold, wet winter in the Rockies gave Steve Young his first taste of what the next dozen years would provide him in various forms.

During Young's freshman year, Jim McMahon was BYU's starting quarterback. McMahon, who went on to break more than seventy NCAA records, was poised to deliver the Cougars their first bowl victory ever, a thrilling comeback win over Southern Methodist in the 1980 Holiday Bowl. McMahon's backup was senior Royce Bybee. Behind Bybee was the heir apparent, Eric Krzmarzick; next in the pecking order at "Quarterback U.," were Mark Haugo, Gym Kimball, and Mike Jones. Then Young.

Steve Young in a typical pose outside the pocket.

The first summer during two-a-days in Provo was anything but magic for the man who had been called the Magician. It was very tough. Young was lost in the shuffle. When the first home game arrived in September against San Diego State, Young opened his locker to get ready for the game and there was no jersey hanging there. A jersey in your locker meant you would dress for the game. Young would go to the game dressed in street clothes and hang around the sidelines.

The next week he played in a junior varsity game at Snow Junior College in Ephraim, Utah. Kimball and Haugo played before Young got his chance, which came late in the game. Young turned some broken plays into some big gains. In the closing minutes of the game he scored a two-point conversion on a quarterback keeper that won the game.

Despite this performance, Young's status on the varsity team did not change. He still did not dress for the next home game and he was not put on the traveling squad.

To make matters worse, at the end of the year, Edwards called Young into his office and suggested that he might be moved from offense to defense. In other words, perhaps he couldn't cut it at the country's top passing school. Young was in the middle of a winter of discontent.

Doug Scovil, the BYU offensive coordinator whom McMahon and others looked upon as a kind of guru and genius, had looked at Young earlier that year and suggested to Edwards that Young be moved out of his stable and over to the defense, playing free safety. Young's passes were wobbly. The first day tightend Gordon Hudson saw Young at practice, he saw the freshman back-peddle, trip, and fall down. "Who is this guy, a walk-on?" thought Hudson who laughed. Young threw off his back foot. And he was left-handed. BYU players were not used to seeing a lefty pilot their high-octane offense from the wrong side. Young had great speed, but Scovil was afraid

30

Young would never be more than a bailout, run-oriented quarterback on a team that lived by the drop-back pro system of throwing the football.

Quarterback coach Ted Tollner, however, was not sold on the idea that Young should be shipped to the defense. Every time he saw Young tossing footballs to his friends in the Smith Fieldhouse the February of his freshman year, something about the young, curly-haired quarterback remained etched in his mind.

Using Young on defense did make some sense, however. He and Lloyd Jones were the fastest players on the team. Jones was a receiver, and Young's speed could come in handy in the secondary. Besides, why waste Young for three years as a backup quarterback. Edwards had a decision to make. As spring practice began, Tollner kept his ideas for Young alive.

"LaVell just couldn't fathom a quarterback running as fast as me," Young remembers. "It didn't make sense to him. He felt he was loaded at quarterback, so his was pretty logical reasoning to play me at safety."

Tollner, however, continued to lobby for Steve Young. He was convinced that Young was their man. While Young worked out all winter as a defensive back, keeping his mouth shut, he also spent some time throwing the ball and working on his drop-back moves. He worked out like a man possessed. His speed had increased from a 4.6 time in forty yards to a blazing 4.43 which made him a dangerous weapon. Young worked on his steps. He watched film; tried to learn. Tollner also saw that for 30 yards, Young was developing into a deadly accurate passer. Young would watch film, throw, run—everything he could to get better and gain an edge over the competition. Tollner saw in him a leader, an athlete with drive, and a quarterback with a quick release and uncanny reflexes.

When Scovil left BYU to become the head coach at San Diego State, Tollner replaced him as offensive coordinator. Tollner told Edwards he wanted Young. More than fifteen years later, after Steve Young has received All-America accolades, a runner-up finish in the Heisman Trophy voting, the Most Valuable Player in Super Bowl XXIX, and is recognized as the most accurate college and NFL passer of all-time, Ted Tollner appears to have made a good decision.

"I have learned," said Young years later, "you never disprove the doubters. People want to see you prove yourself, all you've got to do is keep backing them up. If they're backing up, then you're doing a great job. I don't think there's ever a moment when they are just going to finally fall down, but as long as I have them backing up, I think I'm doing all right."

The following year Young found himself with Krzmarzick as the backup quarterbacks behind McMahon. In just twelve months he'd managed to turn aside other challengers and convince many doubters he would be a force to be dealt with. Bybee graduated. Krzmarzick later transferred to Florida. Haugo transferred to San Diego State. Kimball transferred to Utah State, and Mike Jones left to play at Cal-Lutheran. Neither Krzmarzick nor Haugo played major roles in their respective schools after leaving BYU. Jones did turn in some numbers at Cal-Lutheran for a young coach named Mike Shepherd. Kimball never made a major impact at Utah State, although he was a great athlete.

Young started three games for BYU during his sophomore year when McMahon got injured in the middle of the Colorado State game. Young entered that game and ran for 61 yards while completing four of ten passes for 63 yards and two touchdowns. The following week he was more impressive in leading the Cougars to a Top 10 ranking with a win over Utah State. He ran 21 times for 63 yards and completed 21 of 40 passes for

Colorado State Rams get a
good view of Steve Young's back.

307 yards and one touchdown. Before each game he threw up. He was wound up so tight he thought he would explode. His final start of the year was an offensive barrage against the University of Nevada at Las Vegas. Although he completed 21 of 40 passes for 269 yard and rushed for 66 more, he threw four interceptions and the Cougars lost. McMahon was back in the lineup the next week against San Diego State. Young's debut was over. He had shown signs of brilliance as a running quarterback, but he also proved to be a very solid passer—a guy with a respectable arm, a quarterback with promise.

More importantly, he never quit. He never accepted the idea that being something else, or allowing others to determine his future, was an acceptable way of life for him. If he walked and talked like a quarterback, he was a quarterback. And nobody could sell him a bag of goods. If quarterbacks are the peacocks of football, he proved he belonged with the pretty birds.

In the ensuing months, Young found himself tasting stardom. Because he was a direct descendent of Brigham Young, newspapers across the country picked up on the novelty. He had a built-in gimmick going for himself. And with his black curly hair, blue eyes, and Madison Avenue public relations approach to media interviews he was immediately a media favorite. He appeared on "Good Morning America" with David Hartman. He almost seemed to glow on camera.

The fall of 1981 America discovered Steve Young. Although his performances on the field had been brief, he'd shown enough to start himself on a course that would change his life forever. The stage was set for his junior year. He would be the starting quarterback at BYU. A legend was in the making.

In the course of the next football season, Young worked his way into BYU's quarterback factory, taking it by storm. He captured the imagination of college football fans across the country. He dressed in Levis, wore T-shirts, and had trademark floppy-laced tennis shoes. As the BYU starter his junior year, he completed 230 of 367 passes (a whopping 62 percent) for 3,507 yards while running for 407 more. He was responsible for 28 BYU touchdowns that year and his name was constantly mentioned with reference to All-America honors. Yet he drove a 1965 Oldsmobile with more than 200,000 miles on the odometer. The Olds had been Grit's car which he sent to Provo for Steve and Mike to use at school.

Throughout the coming years that old Olds would become a symbol of the Young ethic. It was old, but it was dependable. It had been taken care of by Grit, who had worked on it himself, babying the old car through the years, refusing to let it quit. He'd taught his kids the value of taking care of things. The Olds was not flashy according to the standards of a world where BMWs and Porches flew by the mile markers on the freeway. But during the next decade that Olds would be the subject of stories by the nation's top sportswriters and broadcasters. Somehow it always seemed appropriate story material. That old car said a lot about Steve Young.

"Death hath a thousand doors to let out life."—Phillip Massinger

LIFE IS A GIFT

Young people often see themselves as invincible, immune from the powers that can take life away. But death is omnipresent and young lives do not always escape its viselike grip. On April 23, 1983, a day that changed their lives forever, Steve Young, Eric Nunn, and Jill Simmons learned about death on Interstate 80 in Nebraska. In broad daylight on a dry road under sunny skies all three could have died. Only two survived when the car in which they were riding rolled over.

Friday April 22 marked the end of the school year at Brigham Young University in the wet and rainy spring of 1983 in Provo, Utah. Jill Simmons, nineteen, made plans to drive home to Scarsdale, New York, and asked a friend, Eric Nunn, from Shelley, Idaho, to accompany her and help with the driving chores. Members of Jill's family were longtime friends with the LeGrande Young family of nearby Greenwich. Steve Young had dated Jill's older sister Torri, so there was little question or debate when Jill's father, Ted, concerned about the safety of the long trip, requested that Steve join the twenty-three-year-old Eric and Jill for the trip home. Ted Simmons was one of those who had called BYU coaches to encourage them to recruit Steve. His persistence helped get the star a scholarship.

Steve, twenty-one years old, had just completed his junior year at BYU. Spring football practice was over and the young athlete was earning recognition as a possible All-America candidate. Eric and Jill had just finished their freshman year. They had planned a trip to Scarsdale and intended to explore New York City for Nunn's benefit. Nunn and Simmons were close friends, nothing more. They were just two students, ready to escape for the summer and put final exams behind them.

On Friday night Eric and Jill attended a wedding reception in Salt Lake City for mutual friends. The plan called for Steve to meet them at the reception. It was 10 p.m. at night before they piled into Simmons's Chevrolet Citation and headed up Parley's Canyon through Park City towards Wyoming on I-80. Steve started driving, with Eric in the front and Jill taking the back seat.

The trio drove into the night and stopped at a gas station in Wyoming, filling up the gas tank and changing drivers. Eric took the wheel, with Jill coming up front. Steve Young quickly fell asleep. The game plan called for one person to stay awake with the driver while the third slept in the back. "I tried to get Jill to sleep when she was in the back, but she wouldn't. She wanted to stay up. When she got in the front seat with me, she didn't sleep but tried to keep me awake by talking," remembers Eric, who drove the eastern portion of Wyoming, through Laramie and Cheyenne. The car was set on cruise control at 70 miles per hour.

The traveling party pulled into North Platte, Nebraska, the following morning, having traveled almost to the halfway point of that state. Eric was exhausted after eating breakfast but wanted to continue driving. Jill had not slept all night. Steve made the executive decision that he would drive some more and Eric crawled into the back seat and fell asleep.

Eric woke up to the sound of Steve and Jill laughing. The car was on cruise control, there was no traffic, but the car was slightly swaying down the freeway as Steve and Jill were exchanging places. With Steve holding the wheel, Jill had crawled onto his lap as he slid to the passenger seat; she then took control of the vehicle, pointing it towards Kearney, some 75 miles from North Platte.

Once settled into the driver's seat, Jill turned around and apologized to the dreary-looking Eric in the back seat. "I'm sorry for dragging you along."

"No, you guys are going to have a tremendous time in New York," said Steve. "Just tremendous."

Eric slumped back into his back seat roost and quickly fell asleep. The next thing he knew, he was laying in a wheat field, groggy and slipping in and out of consciousness, confused over what was reality and what was a dream.

Moments earlier, Steve Young had snapped out of a daze looked over at Jill and discovered that she had fallen asleep Steve lunged for the wheel, attempting to take control of the car, which was careening towards the shoulder of the freeway. It was too late.

One report indicated that the vehicle turned over six times. During one of those revolutions, Jill fell halfway out of the car, her head trapped between the ground and the outside top of the car. None of the three youths was wearing a seat belt. In the ensuing hour, Steve encountered perhaps the most horribly frustrating experience of his life. He tried reviving Jill by giving her CPR. He also tried with futility to flag down passing motorists. It was nearly noon. Nobody would stop. Not one car pulled over and offered any help to the three survivors. Jill was critically injured. Motorists on

I-80 just kept going by. Nearly forty five minutes passed before an ambulance arrived at the scene.

Eric woke up in the emergency room of Good Samaritan Hospital in Kearney, Nebraska, and aides told him Jill Simmons was dead. "I didn't know how to feel. I was numb. It didn't seem real."

A few minutes later Steve entered the room, his eyes glazed over. He looked wrung out, tired and distant.

"Jill is gone," Steve mumbled. "She's gone."

"I know, Steve. I know. She was ready to go," Eric muttered, gathering himself.

"She was ready," said Steve. "If it were me or you, I'd be afraid. But this girl was a saint, an angel. I don't worry about her because she is in a better place. I know she is happy. She is always happy. How bad are you hurt?"

Eric Nunn was not seriously hurt. He had a gash on his head which required stitches and doctors kept him overnight. Steve Young had a cut on his wrist and was shaken up. He took a flight home immediately.

Two weeks later, after Jill Simmons's funeral, Eric Nunn got a call from Steve Young. "I just had to call. You were there," said the quarterback, who had barely known Nunn before the accident. With his voice breaking and tears beginning to flow, he continued. "I just had to call. I know you understand."

Steve and Eric talked about what had happened that day. Eric remembered only a little.

"I didn't know where you were," Steve told Eric of the scene. "I didn't think about you. All I wanted to do is help Jill."

In the months that followed there were other phone calls between the two men. There were a lot of tears. "We were grieving. We were going through a process we needed," remembers Eric.

"Whenever I turn on the TV and see Steve Young, I remember that day and I remember Jill," says Eric. "Perhaps we survived for a purpose. We were given a second chance here. We could have been dead, too. I remember that we are alive for a reason. Steve says we have some things to do and that's why we are still here. I've gained a lot of respect for Steve over the years. You never know when it is your time to go, or when you will be taken. Steve has been a gentleman and a great human being. There is no air of superiority about him. He was just trying to enjoy life then, and he's just trying to make something of his life now. Jill Simmons was an example for both of us, both in life and death. Steve and I are trying to be more like Jill."

Nunn and Young learned many lessons they will never forget on that April day in 1983. One of the lessons learned on the plains of Nebraska was that life is a precious possession, not something to be wasted.

"I will never forget it as long as I live," says Young. "It changed my life forever."

"Whether you believe you can, or believe you cannot, you are right." — *Robert L. Backman*

PERSPECTIVE

Imagine living the life of Steve Young in 1983. You are an All-American college quarterback, handsome, popular, a top candidate for the Heisman Trophy. Experts project that you will make millions in the NFL. The media loves you. The fans adore you. Everyone thinks you are bound for a life of dreams and glory. The world appears to be at your doorstep and all you have to do is reach for the knob.

Lesser men would and have rushed to that portal, indulging themselves up to their eyeballs in the good life, drinking in fame and gorging themselves on the adoration of the masses. A few, like Steve Young, tried to get a grip on what seemed to them more like a runaway train, before it dragged them down the tracks.

Steve Young looked fame in the face. It scared him to death.

Young had earned the starting quarterback spot at BYU. He carried the weight of replacing college football legends—All-Americans. At times perhaps he wished that somebody would come by and blow up the stadium so he wouldn't have to go out and perform and be compared to others. He vomited

Steve Young launches a long one
against the New Mexico Lobos.

before and during every game. He was wound as tight as a golf ball. And there was nothing to do about it but play.

It all started with his junior year in 1982 when Young led BYU to a Western Athletic Conference championship and an 8–4 record. When he took the Cougars to a 17–12 win over Utah to clinch the championship, he allowed himself to believe he had arrived, that he had replaced the great Jim McMahon and put the other BYU quarterback ghosts behind him.

Coach LaVell Edwards recognized Young's potential just in the way he approached life and thought about his job on the field. "I remember the second game he ever played in as a starter. We were at the University of Georgia and they had just won a national championship. The stadium there in Athens is one of the toughest places in the country to play, with 82,000 people, and it is raining a little bit. As we go off the field at halftime the score was 7–7 and Steve had thrown five interceptions. As the team walked towards the locker room I thought to myself that we have a good chance of winning this game. I think what I need to do is to get Steve off to the side and get him pepped up and not let him get down on himself. If I can keep him up, we can beat Georgia. So I go over to Steve off to the side and start talking to him and before I can even get halfway through what I had to say, he looked at me and said: 'Hey, coach, there is no problem. There is no problem here. Don't worry, there is no problem here.' And I think to myself, 'what does he mean there is no problem? Hey dummy, you just threw five interceptions and there is no problem?' But that is the way he thought."

Edwards got another dose of Young in the final game of his junior year. BYU played in the 1982 Holiday Bowl against Ohio State. "We're playing against a very, very good football team, maybe the best team we'd ever faced. And we were getting beat about as bad as a football team could be beaten. And the game is down to a minute left and the score is something like 47–17. Steve dropped back to pass and was looking for somebody to throw to and one of the Ohio State players came in and hit him as hard as I've ever seen a player get hit. He fell to the ground, his helmet went one way and he went the other. The blow knocked the wind out of him. Steve laid on the ground and held onto the ball. We had to call time out while the trainers went on to the field and revived him. We got him up and brought him to the sidelines. We put in a replacement quarterback to run a couple of plays. Then I feel a tap on my shoulder and I turn around and it is Steve," said Edwards.

"Coach, I have to go back in," said Young.

Edwards looked at Young and told him he had to be out of his mind. "With the hit you just took and we're getting beat?"

"Coach. I gotta go back in. I know they are going to win the game. But I don't want them to ever believe that they beat me, that they got the better of me," said the quarterback.

"So I send him in the game. We have only one or two more plays left. We're behind. He drops back, completes a pass that goes to the two-yard line, and time on the clock runs out. Steve goes over and shakes peoples' hands, congratulates them and then runs off the field for the locker room with his head up."

"As I thought about that and remember looking at that on the sidelines, I remember seeing other players on the team sitting on the bench with their heads in their hands. We had other guys talking to people in the stands. There were a lot of people on our team just waiting for it to end so they could get out of there. But here was Steve, he knew there was a game that needed to be played and that he had to be a part of it. What that proved to me is that a lot in life depends on how you look at it. Steve always looked at his role and his job as something he had to do and give his best for. Right up to the end, whether winning or losing, you have to finish it."

46

Playing against the Cowboys and the
refs in Laramie Wyoming.

Young's Senior year was a memorable one for BYU fans. The passing attack of the Cougars was always exciting to watch but Steve Young seemed to add another dimension to the action on the field. One memorable game which really showed everyone what Young was made of took place October 29, 1983, Cougar Stadium, Provo, Utah, before a sellout crowd of 64,593. BYU was playing instate rival Utah State and on this Saturday afternoon the Aggies were not about to lay down for the favored and more visible Cougars. The series had turned a little ugly during the 80s, with fights and a ton of penalties.

The Aggies were leading 21-17 just before halftime. On the last drive of the half, BYU was deep in Aggie territory and was looking for a score to go into the locker room ahead by a field goal. Young dropped back but was knocked mercilessly hard to the turf just after letting a regrettable pass float into the grasp of a Utah State cornerback. As the Aggie sprinted, for what was to everyone watching, a sure touchdown, Young jumped to his feet and chased him down the length of the field and caught him from behind, preventing the score. It was one of the greatest feats of athleticism most fans had ever seen. Young was then pulled from the game suffering with a concussion which was the result of the sack *before* his inspiring tackle. In the waning minutes of the game Young, cleared to return to the game, led BYU 67 yards in the final two minutes and scored the winning touchdown with 11 seconds on the clock. Young later said he could not remember his spectacular tackle or few other plays in the game. But the fans at that game remember.

The BYU Cougars were having a great year. Young caught the imagination of the college football world as he teamed up with tight end Gordon Hudson and the two attacked the record books.

Young and Hudson were featured in *Sports Illustrated* as a passing duo to be reckoned with in college football. The magazine story, entitled "The Steve and Gordon Show," painted a picture of the two stars, their life on campus as roommates, and the terror they brought opposing defenders on the field. The two battled each other constantly, arguing over everything: women, studies, sports, attitudes—you name it.

"A nice conversation between us is an argument," Young told writer Jack McCallum. They even fought over who would answer the phone. "We'd sit there yelling at each other until it stopped ringing." But they were best friends. And there has rarely been a more potent passing combination in college football. Together they gave the Cougars a very successful year which included a close and exciting win over UCLA in Pasadena.

Their last game together remains etched in the memories of Cougar fans. BYU earned the right to compete in the 1983 Holiday Bowl against the University of Missouri. BYU had also earned the dubious distinction of consistently capping great seasons with a bowl loss, and Missouri was sure they would be able to help the Cougars live down to their past.

The game featured BYU's potent offense against Missouri's stingy defense and for almost the entire game Missouri's defense won out. Then, with Missouri leading BYU 17–14 and one minute left in the game, Young led the Cougars from their own seven-yard line to the Missouri fifteen. On first down, the call came from coach Norm Chow in the press box down to quarterback coach Mike Holmgren It was a fake sweep run and throw back to the quarterback—a trick play BYU had seldom practiced and never used in a game. Young surveyed the defense as he came to the line of scrimmage. Sure enough, Missouri was playing man coverage in the secondary, like they had most of the game. If the safety cheated and came to the line of scrimmage, he might not think to cover the quarterback after the handoff to the fullback.

Young handed off to Eddie Stinnett, who started running the sweep to the right side of the field. The Missouri safety bit on the play, moving over to help make a tackle. After handing off the ball, Young squirted out into the left flat, away from the flow of the play. Stinnett suddenly stopped, turned and lofted the ball down the other side of the field towards Young. Stinnett had led Young with the ball and the quarterback used a last-second spurt of speed to get to the falling football, which sailed just over the outstretched arms of a Missouri player who had recovered from the fake a split-second too late.

Young caught the ball on a dead run and crossed the goal line for the winning touchdown. Young then did something that later shocked even himself. He started pumping his legs in a sort of Indian rain dance, holding the ball over his head. Young, the ultimate "Up Tight One," let loose and lost a little control. It was a new feeling for Young; he wasn't used to such an outburst from himself.

That moment is cemented in the minds of BYU fans. It was the last time they saw the popular quarterback playing for the Cougars. That year, Young finished second in the Heisman Trophy voting to Nebraska's Mike Rozier.

When his college career ended, Young had led Brigham Young to a 11–1 record, a national ranking, a bowl victory, and a conference championship. He set an NCAA record for pass completion percentage in a season (1983, 306 of 429, 71.3 percent) and in a career (1981–83, 592 of 908, 65.2 percent). Those marks are still in the NCAA books. He also was named among the NCAA's top scholar athletes.

Gil Brandt, the player personnel director for the Dallas Cowboys, was quoted as saying of Young: "How good is he? LaVell Edwards may not admit this, but I think he's the best

Holiday Bowl vs. Missouri
Young's TD catch part one

Holiday Bowl vs. Missouri
Young's TD catch part two

Holiday Bowl vs. Missouri
Young's TD catch part three

they've had there. And he's the most accurate passer I've ever seen. Period." Nearly a decade after Young's college career ended, *Sports Illustrated* ranked the top college quarterbacks of the past. Douglas Looney in the 1991 Fall special issue used a unique formula to evaluate the players. Looney applied the formula to fifty of the best, using yards per attempt, completion percentage, touchdowns minus interceptions, yards per rushing attempt, average yards per play, and winning percentage. Steve Young rated No. 1, followed by Jim McMahon and Robbie Bosco (who followed Young at BYU), then Vinnie Testaverde from the University of Miami.

At the end of his college career in Provo, Young got the message from scouts and agents. He was hot. He was going to be a millionaire and he needed to start thinking about how he'd spend the money. Few things could have bothered Young more. He didn't like people thinking he was spoiled and rich and had gobs of money hanging around. Steve knew where he'd been and where he had come from. If he went home, he knew Grit would make him take out the garbage, mow the lawn, and even help Tom or Jim do the newspaper route.

The thought of all Grit had taught him about work and values had a comfortable ring to it. It felt right. For that reason, Young very methodically set about to remain himself, to retain what threads of his life he could. The other things would come and go. He had once left home for Provo and stood as the number eight quarterback on the depth chart. He would not forget what tracks he had left behind.

That was pretty mature thinking for a potential superstar. It was a rarity in the world of high-power sports, drenched in lucrative contracts.

Young was ready to graduate with a dual major in international business and finance after just seven semesters of school. He wanted to go to law school. As the day approached

BYU's win vs. UCLA

when he would step out of the ranks of amateur college athletics, Young kept wearing Levis, driving the old Oldsmobile, and going on double and triple dates with Hudson and other college buddies and their girlfriends. A fun night in Provo for this bunch included riding around, listening to Bruce Springsteen music, a movie, and pizza.

As 1983 came to a close Young was getting a taste of what was ahead. As he would learn even more in years to come, everybody wanted a piece of him. Weird stuff started to happen. Letters poured in from all over the country and continued to pour in through the decade as he entered professional football. The letters even included proposals of marriage from young women and their parents. People sent in stuff to be signed. The BYU football office established a procedure to handle Steve Young correspondence; secretary Shirley Johnson took on the job.

Young had a problem: not only was he a great athlete, handsome, and soon to be rich, but God had blessed him with the ability to stand up before an audience and deliver very articulate and moving speeches. Although he was shy by nature, he was as natural a speaker as any presidential candidate. When he got behind a podium, people listened. They would sometimes cry. Reporters who interviewed him needed notebooks, pens, and microphones out quick—if they were late, they'd surely miss a sound bite or good quote.

Whenever Young needed a break, he would hide out at the home of Doug and Barbara Schaerrer or the eight-acre horse ranch in Provo owned by Jim Burr. The Burr home became a refuge for Young during his junior and senior years. He would use it as a hideout from the media and others demanding his time. Many years afterwards, when the Burrs encountered some financial problems, Young bought the ranch. He didn't know anything about horses; but it was the right thing to do.

56

Steve Young at the Holiday Bowl
practicing for a long career of press interviews .

Within a few weeks Young would be a millionaire. He couldn't help but wonder how high the price tag would be. Within weeks the answer came. He would become known as the forty-million dollar man, his name linked to the richest contract in pro sports. He was just 22 years old. "I almost fainted that day," he recalled. "I remember talking to Channel 5 in Los Angeles and I had to hold on to the rail. I was overwhelmed. It was unbelievable."

*"Were does the ant die except in
sugar?" —Maylay Proverb."*

MILLIONS IN THE POCKET

In March 1984 Steve Young found himself on the auc-
tion block, merchandise, something to be bargained for, bid on,
and sold. In ancient times, he could be a gladiator. In modern
times, he was to become a professional athlete.

Young had a series of important decisions to make following his college football career. With what agent would he
sign to represent him? Would he play in the new upstart United
States Football League or in the National Football League? And
how much should he settle for if there were offers and counter-
offers on the table?

Young chose agent Leigh Steinberg, one of the most
respected professional athlete representatives in the country.
Together they decided on the USFL, which promised to make
Young one of the first players taken in its draft. Once Young
was chosen by the Los Angeles Express as the tenth pick of the
USFL draft, Steinberg worked on completing the deal. And what
a deal it turned out to be.

Steinberg had practiced sports law for more than twenty years. A chief partner in the California law firm of Steinberg & Moorad, he has a client list of more than 100 athletes, including professional football, basketball, baseball and hockey players. He has represented the first player selected in five of the last six NFL drafts prior to 1995: Troy Aikman, Jeff George, Russell Maryland, Drew Bledsoe and Dan Wilkinson.

One March morning Young left classes at BYU, went to his apartment and changed into some nicer clothes, hopped in the barge—the Oldsmobile—and headed for the Provo airport. There he boarded a private jet and headed for the world of corporate sports where money ran like honey. Young was headed for a meeting with forty-six-year-old Bill Oldenburg, owner of Investment Mortgage International Inc., at his office in San Francisco. Oldenburg was the owner of the Los Angeles Express, the starship franchise of the United States Football League. The USFL wanted to steal as many college football players as it could from the NFL. The new league needed TV ratings so it could get TV money and with that money it could challenge the grand-daddy league for talent and air time—and succeed. The USFL wanted college's best. The league wanted Steve Young and Nebraska's Heisman Trophy winner Mike Rozier. Cost was a mere formality.

Young arrived in San Francisco and got in a limo which pointed towards downtown San Francisco and that attractive pyramid shaped building that overlooks the bay. Young and Steinberg entered Oldenburg's office suites featuring Italian marble floors, Chinese antiques, Brazilian rosewood paneling, and gold-ornamented artifacts. A plush carpet cushioned their feet.

They were on fairly high ground. The USFL wanted Young. Oldenburg wanted Young. Steinberg knew their position, and the cost would be high. In the ensuing hours the parties would negotiate and sign what at that time was the most lucrative contract in the history of organized team sports. Don Klosterman, a very astute businessman, had already pounded out the key details with Steinberg and Grit Young. All that was needed were a few stipulations and specific riders to the pact. Yet those little nagging details kept the party of Young and the party of Oldenburg face-to-face most of the afternoon, and then into the night and early morning of the next day.

The basic deal called for a four-year contract with the Express, which included a signing bonus of $2.5 million, a no-interest loan of up to $1.5 million, a $275,000 bonus for coming to training camp when required to be there, a base salary for the season of $1.9 million, a clause establishing a $183,000 scholarship fund at BYU, and an escalating annuity plan which would provided $34.5 million to Young through the year 2027. In all, the contract was worth a whopping $40.1 million, a figure that would stop the presses at newspapers around the world.

Steinberg insisted that Young receive the guaranteed parts of the deal immediately—as in now. Oldenburg was getting more and more testy; it was his birthday and he had already missed his own party plans with family and friends. Oldenburg was used to snapping his fingers and having things done; but Steinberg still wanted the guarantees in cash.

Steinberg was concerned that the USFL and the Express were big talkers, that they wanted the college stars, but would protect themselves more than the star athletes if the new league had to bail out. Steinberg's fears would later become reality.

"You want guarantees?" Oldenburg barked out at one point in the talks. "Here's all the guarantees you'll need." And with that he grabbed and wadded up a fist full of big bills on his desk, throwing them on the floor in front of Young.

Later that night, Oldenburg walked over to Young and, with his finger, poked the college star in the chest, letting him know he didn't appreciate Young's refusal to sign the deal as it stood before the meeting.

Young, puzzled, frustrated, and angry, recoiled: "If you touch me again, I'll deck you."

The talks screeched to a halt. Oldenburg didn't want to shell out greenbacks right out of his pocket, he'd rather create the deal with some paper. Steinberg wanted Young to get what he was worth and didn't want checks that might bounce. Oldenburg finally ordered security to throw out Steinberg and Young. A few days later Steinberg and Klosterman hammered out the deal and Young became a member of the Express.

Headlines across the country screamed out the figure, $40 million. A debate ensued. Who in the world was worth $40 million? By standards of the 1990s, such a contract is almost routine. But ten years earlier it was considered excessive and a little obscene. Uptight as usual, Young worried about the deal, the money, and the fallout that followed across the country not to mention the reaction of his future teammates. Besides shucking off would-be tacklers and throwing pinpoint passes, Young was an expert worrier.

Even though the experts in the NFL put him on a pedestal; Young didn't like it. Said Dallas Cowboys' Gil Brandt: "He's a definite number one pick. If you could somehow measure what one player means to a team, Steve Young would be the most valuable player in college football today." And then, there was this monster contract. And it was unloaded right on worry wart Steve Young's head.

Steve Young with his new owner, Bill Oldenburg.

In 1984 here's how the world of sports salaries stood:

Athlete	Team	Pay	Years
1. Steve Young	L.A. Express	$40 Million	43 years
2. Magic Johnson	L.A. Lakers	$25 Million	25 years
3. Dave Winfield	N.Y. Yankees	$21 Million	10 years
4. Wayne Gretzky	Edmonton Oilers	$21 Million	21 years
5. Larry Bird	Boston Celtics	$15 Million	7 years
6. Gary Carter	Montreal Expos	$15 Million	8 years
7. Moses Malone	Philadelphia 76ers	$13 Million	6 years
8. George Foster	N.Y. Mets	$10 Million	5 years

Although Young might be shackled to the same employer for longer than the other athletes, the $40 million was more money than a lot of living legends were making.

"From the money aspect we were overwhelmed," Steinberg told reporters the day of the official signing.

But before Young took a pen out and signed, he received calls from NFL commissioner Pete Rozelle and his lifetime idol, Dallas Cowboy quarterback Roger Staubach, who told him to sign with the NFL and go to Cincinnati. Donald Trump, owner of the USLF's New Jersey Generals and the late broadcaster Howard Cosell called and told him to try the USFL. He decided upon the latter. Steinberg and Young had rejected an offer of $3.5 million over five years from the Cincinnati Bengals, who had the No. 1 pick in the upcoming May draft.

Oldenburg would have to make huge deferred payments to Young in the coming years. While Oldenburg would be liable for payments to Young through the year 2027, Young would only have to play for Oldenburg's Express for four years. It was astounding.

"I don't see how they can possibly make it as a league by doing these kinds of things. They better be rich," said Brandt of the Cowboys. "In my wildest imagination, I don't see how anybody can do this and stay in business. Maybe they know something nobody else does."

Some befuddlement and outrage followed the Young deal. Even USFL commissioner Chet Simmons, who wanted to hold salaries down, expressed disappointment it had gone as far as it had. "The idea was to be reasonable. Then came the competition. Once it starts, it's tough as hell to stop it. As commissioner I don't like it. It worries me. I do not think it is in the best interest of professional football or the league, but what is to be done? These are wealthy businessmen seeking to build and sell a product and to compete."

Young found himself in the center of a philosophical firestorm.

William Dunavant Jr., owner of the USFL's Memphis Showboats, called the Young deal ridiculous. "I can't conceive of anything like this. We want to be competitive, but this doesn't make economic sense at all."

Klosterman admitted that the Express did not look to make a financial windfall with such deals. "We're looking for exposure. That is the important thing. We made a commitment to put together the best possible team, and we're right on the road to do that."

In reality, Young's deal had big numbers, but it was really not a lot different from the USFL's deals with Heisman Trophy winners Herschel Walker (Georgia) and Mike Rosier (Nebraska). On an annual salary schedule, it was comparable. Oldenburg told reporters at the Beverly Hills Hilton on signing day that Young was only getting market value. "The league has talked about going head-to-head with the NFL in the fall," Oldenburg said. "And the NFL talked about going head-to-head

65

with us (for players) in the spring. Well, they've lost the first round when we signed this young man."

Steinberg said Young's deal was unlike any he had ever seen. "In terms of upfront money it is better than Warren Moon's [with the Houston Oilers] and better than John Elway's [with the Denver Broncos]. It's the future considerations that make Young's contract extraterrestrial." Young's agent maintained that the money was not the primary factor for his client. "It's funny that the biggest financial commitment in sports goes to the guy who is the least money-hungry that I've ever dealt with." Steinberg, at the time, represented more than fifty athletes in the NFL and thirteen in the USFL.

Steinberg had never encountered anybody like Young. He was the real item, a genuine All-American kid, who walked the walk and was not a phony. For an agent, Young was a gold mine, a person who would bring him millions in years to come. Steinberg was stunned with Young's humility, maturity, and perception. When Young got his $2.5 million signing-bonus check, he flipped it to Steinberg saying: "Here, you take it. I don't want it."

"If you get to know Steve Young, sit down and talk with him for more than five minutes, you'll see a person who genuinely wants to help people," said his agent.

Young appeared before the media a little stunned. He stood before the country's press, and, fighting back his bashful nature, told reporters he hadn't expected a fortune for playing. "Crud, I just wanted enough to fix my car and take my girl-friend out to dinner, which I haven't been able to do except for McDonald's."

Nobody believed him. Except those who knew him.

Nothing in his life had ever been about money. And now he could have almost anything he wanted, a fact that would trigger exhilaration in most male Americans. Heck, in virtually

Steve Young with his agent Leigh Steinberg
going over 40 million details.

everybody. But not in Young. After returning to Provo to wrap up affairs before reporting to the Los Angeles Express training camp, he began to feel the weight of what had happened. It scared him. He worried about his values. He wondered if he would continue to see things the same way—the way they made sense. He worried whether people, his friends, would treat him differently, or if those same movie-and-pizza nights would go on just as usual. Would he ever have a relationship with a girl based on just being him and the girl being just herself? Or would it be the money? And, if he bought a new car, how would he be perceived? Would he feel different about himself, about others, about his faith in God?

It would be safe to say that Steve Young was among the few sports heroes in history to worry so deep and so long about so much the day after becoming a millionaire. "I had times to-day when I wanted to give it all back," Young told a *Los Angeles Examiner* newspaper columnist.

Steve called his father one night after the signing and told him he was seriously thinking about calling the whole deal off. "The money just overwhelmed him," said Grit. "The money became his nemesis and he continued to live as if he didn't have it. He told me before he had to report to camp. 'I don't want to go.' I ended up having to go out to Provo and talk to him. I told him, 'You made a contract; you live up to the contract.'"

Steve told one reporter: "I'm worrying about my values and I keep coming up negative. Right now I'm a guy having a lot of trouble handling this. This spot is too much for me. Maybe I'm the wrong guy to be in this position." Although that kind of talk might sound corny, it was pure and simple Steve Young. He had experienced order in his life. Now he had chaos.

Young said, "When I decided to sign with the Express, it was late. I had promised to give them an answer within a certain time-frame. I'd been up for two days straight. It seemed the best thing to do under the circumstances. I am at the press conference and I'm sweating. I'm thinking, What am I doing here? I'm sure many people don't understand this money. I don't either. On the plane afterward, it was a private plane, just me and my girlfriend, I cried all the way home."

The fallout over the Young deal was quite like the star collegian thought and feared it might be. Cincinnati Bengal coach Sam Wyche told the Associated Press that the Young contract was bad for the game. Yet Young wanted to do what was right, not what was wrong for sports. He told one interviewer that people rarely consider something when they dream of striking it rich—how it affects perspective. "To me, the challenges in life are what makes it exciting. Half the fun of life is being insecure, wondering if you can make it. The fun is in the earning of your achievement."

Young tried to sleep that week, trying to clarify in his mind what money was and what it wasn't. He came to the conclusion that he would ignore the money and just try to do his job. He couldn't control what other people thought, but he could control what he thought and did. From that day on, Steve Young continued to wear Levis and tennis shoes. He took his signing-bonus check and put it in the pocket of his jeans, where it was found wadded up more than a week later. He continued to drive around the old Oldsmobile that looked somewhat like a tuna boat and was about as easy to park as a panzer tank. That old car had been nursed by his father for more than sixteen years. Steve Young would not buy his first brand new sticker car, a Jeep, for another three years. It was a symbolic thing, an exercise in self discipline.

He did do one thing out of character, but it was not for himself. He gave Grit money for a new Corvette, something his frugal father had always wanted. Grit refused the money. He shuffled the money to his other children for college tuition instead. More than ten years later Grit finally bought a red convertible Corvette.

"We were shocked," said Steve, who had inherited his father's frugality. He then joked: "Grit told the neighbors that it was a rental and refused to drive it to church."

*"I will ignore the obstacles at my feet and
keep mine eyes on the goals above my head,
for I know that where dry desert ends, green
grass grows."* —Og Mandino

DEALING WITH EXPECTATIONS

The nickname came quick and stuck for a long, long time. Steve Young became known as the $40 million man. He hated it.

"To say he had a hard time with that is a major understatement," remembers George Curtis, head trainer of the Los Angeles Express, who befriended Young and, like most trainers, worked not only on his physical pains but also his emotional wounds. "Steve struggled with the $40 million label because he worried about what people were saying. There were a lot of people, national media guys, football players and fans who criticized the contract and the criticism hit Steve hard. He fretted. He worried. And it made him sick."

If people know you are making $40 million, you automatically become a target to some. Every move you make is scrutinized. That made Young's debut as a professional even tougher. And Young heaped a lot of pressure on himself, as well.

"Nobody, but nobody was tougher on Steve than he was on himself. I believe you could say that about him all his life, he's always been that way," said Curtis.

If the truth were known, in 1984 the $40 million contract made a lot of headlines, but the Express and Oldenburg would not be around long enough to make those numbers come to fruition. Within two years the USFL would fold and Oldenburg would encounter troubles within his billion-dollar financial empire. The wily Steinberg was right in demanding upfront money from Oldenburg. When the USFL fell apart, that money was all Young came away with—approximately ten percent of the Big Deal.

However, in the spring of 1984 nobody knew that. All they knew was that Steve Young was the USFL's cover boy and that he was going to get $40 million. And for $40 million he'd better be able to leap tall buildings in a single bound.

Young found himself in a very difficult situation. Any rookie quarterback would be hard-pressed to step right into professional football and immediately make an impact. Young not only was expected to do that with the Express and its group of mercenary players, but also was expected to carry the entire league, TV ratings and all. No one man could ever accomplish such a task.

Young joined the Express after the season was already in progress. He would have to get himself ready to play in approximately two weeks and then be moved immediately in as the starter. His coach was former San Diego Charger quarterback John Hadl and his position coach was a passing guru by the name of Sid Gillman.

During Young's first day at practice, he was throwing a skeleton passing drill. He was nervous, pressured. One of his first passes sailed five feet over the head of receiver JoJo Townsend. Young turned and swore; he was mad, embarrassed, and frustrated with himself.

"Hey Steve," said Gillman. "Come over here, would you."

When Steve got near, the coach moved in close so the other players couldn't hear him. "Steve I know you feel some pressure here. I know you're mad because you threw that pass over his head. But Steve, get a grip on yourself. These guys out there are counting on you. They see you as their leader and look to you to guide them. I don't care if you never complete another pass in this drill, act like a leader out there and show them something about leading them."

Thus counseled, Young returned and completed the drill. More than a decade later Young would point to Gillman as one of the most influential people in his life. "I don't know what Sid thinks of me, but I was kind of an erratic, fly-by-night quarterback, and he grabbed me by the throat the first season I was in L.A. and beat into my head that I had to stabilize everything—my game, my life, everything. I was pretty hardheaded even back then, and he was one of the rare people who was more hardheaded than me, so he won. His influence remains, because I thought he was a great man, someone you end up admiring in an overly strange way. He was crusty, ornery and tough, but he was a lovable football coach too. I think he'd seen it all, and I always respected that. The things that he taught me were the things that remained with me throughout that time."

Young joined his teammates the sixth game of the 1984 season. He went on to play twelve games as a rookie. At times he was great, at other times he struggled. More than his share of times he left the pocket, abandoned a play, and took off running. During a game in Chicago on April 20, 1984 he became the first quarterback in professional football history to run for more than 100 yards and pass for more than 300 yards in a single game.

Steve Young scrambles for 13 yards against
the Houston Gamblers.

LA Express' leading rusher Steve Young
with 47 of his 87 yards coming on this TD run.

A victim of a safety blitz, Steve Young is sacked
for a loss vs. the Houston Gamblers.

"I give up!" Steve Young about to be sacked by
the Oakland Invaders' Vito McKeever.

Young lived in Manhattan Beach in Los Angeles with a bunch of roommates. While the Express players had fun, many could tell that the new league was going nowhere fast. Financial difficulties soon hit Oldenburg.

The next season Young played in thirteen of sixteen Express games. By this time the league was suffering under a ton of problems. Oldenburg could not keep his team and the league took over control. A lot of hotel bills went unpaid. One day the Express players found themselves locked out of their practice facilities. Coach Hadl asked players who were from Southern California if teammates could stay at their homes. *Sports Illustrated* published a story of a bus driver pulling over to the side of the road. Worried about getting paid for hauling the team to the final home game of the season, the driver refused to go any farther towards the stadium unless he was immediately paid. Players passed around a hat and Young reportedly put the most money in the kitty. The Express arrived in time to play the Arizona Wranglers.

In a move to save money, many injured players were not replaced. When Mel Gray, the one remaining healthy running back, went down during a game, Steve Young finished his USFL career playing as a running back. Afterwards, Young laughingly told reporters: "It felt like a high school game out there. I was waiting for the cheerleaders to come running off the bus."

Young finished his USFL career with a very average sixteen touchdown passes and twenty-two interceptions. He completed only 54 percent of his passes and did not look like the superstar people expected from a $40 million man. His totals for the 1984 season were 167 of 310 attempts for 2,361 yards passing and 515 yards rushing. The next year he came short of matching those numbers as the Express and the league started running out of gas.

In 1985, towards the end of the USFL's final season, Young made a deal with the Tampa Bay Buccanners of the NFL. The Bucs owned the rights to Young when they took him as their first pick in the supplemental draft in June 1984.

The Bucs may have been the NFL doormat, but at least it was the NFL—not the USFL.

Young's professional football career up to that point had been up and down. He had his moments, but with a struggling organization and inadequate support, he was far from reaching his potential.

Said Gillman of Young during that era: "He was the most talented quarterback in the game, and he was going to be one of the best quarterbacks ever. There was nothing he couldn't do. He could run, and he could throw, and he scored touchdowns. Sometimes his passes would go all over the place, but we got him reading the field so he could get the ball to the right place at the right time." Gillman predicted ten years before it happened that Young would be a Super Bowl quarterback for somebody. "I'd stake my life on it. Steve can throw any kind of pass that needs to be thrown. He can drill it in there, he can lay it in there, he can touch it in there—and on top of that he has tremendous intelligence."

Gillman spent his entire time with Young trying to get him to bridle himself and play with discipline. "Rookie quarterbacks are going to run more than they should because so many damn things happen on the field that they've never seen before. So they tuck the ball under their arms and they run. But as they begin to get comfortable with the blitzes and the dogs and the various coverages downfield and how they can affect pass patterns, they run less and less."

Once Steinberg worked out the details, Young was on his way to Tampa Bay, where he started the final five games for Tampa Bay in 1985. There were reports that Young paid $1.2

million to escape from the Express, with the stipulation that the USFL would pay the remainder of the monster annuity. As it turned out, the USFL died a quick death and never flipped an opening kickoff coin again.

Once again and like most things in his athletic career, switching to the NFL was not an easy endeavor for Steve Young. His name was linked to money. When he got the release from the Express and arrived at Tampa Bay, the NFL veterans looked at Young with side glances and a lot of jealousy.

Young's agreement with Tampa Bay called for a $5.4 million payment over six years. All Tampa Bay wanted from Young was to save the team—just as Express and the USFL had wanted him to play savior the previous year. Young knew this tune; the trouble was, nobody can play this kind of song.

Tampa Bay had lost its first twenty-six games as an expansion team the first two years it was in the NFL. The Bucs then had three playoff appearances under quarterback Doug Williams. However, the team sunk to the cellar once again after Williams left, unhappy over his contract.

On Young's first day in town he was taken to a posh place called Malio's where he was paraded around to V.I.P.s like a prized animal. Young met Dennis and Linda Diaz, owners of the racehorse Spend a Buck; there was also Harry A. Johnson II, president of the Florida state senate and candidate for governor. At another table was Johnson's running-mate, Attorney General Jim Smith. Arriving soon thereafter was Tony Cunningham, fresh from talks with John Bassett in which he proposed to buy the Tampa Bay Bandits of the USFL. Within the hour, Bucs teammates Jeremiah Castille and Jeff Davis came over to shake Young's hand.

Young was eating with Tom McEwen, sports editor of the *Tampa Tribune*. McEwen filled Young in: Tampa Bay was a real hole of a team, a virtual pit. This was just what the new quarterback wanted to hear. He had just made it to the NFL and now was hearing horror stories about how bad his new team stunk.

The next day, Young met the team including the Bucs' starting quarterback, Steve DeBerg, a guy who had been down this path before. A nine-year NFL veteran, DeBerg had lost his starting job at San Francisco to Joe Montana. At Denver, DeBerg had lost his job to John Elway. "Everytime I get in a situation where I'm the established starter, here comes some young superstar," he lamented.

Bucs coach Leeman Bennett did not expect Young to step right in, but it was clear he wanted to develop the free-wheeling and free spirited Young into a straight drop-back passer. The trouble was that the Bucs did not have an offensive line that could consistently deliver the protection needed for the quarterback in that kind of offense. At Tampa Bay, a drop-back quarterback was a sitting duck for blitzing defensive linemen. To stay in the pocket almost meant signing your own death warrant.

Young's presence on the team would also mean adjustments for somebody besides DeBerg. Backup quarterback Alan Risher would be displaced, his future uncertain. His wife was expecting a baby. Risher did not hide his disappointment over the situation, telling reporters: "It's out of my control. There's nothing I can do about it. Steve Young signed for $6 million and he hasn't proved a thing on the field yet. But when you pay that kind of money for somebody, he doesn't have to prove a whole hell of a lot. Guys like me are the ones who struggle to make a football team." Risher was right. That was the business of football.

Young was caught in circumstances beyond his control. To make matters worse, the main person who could help Young adjust and learn the offense at Tampa Bay had a freak accident and was not around. Seven days after Young signed with the Bucs, offensive coordinator Jimmy Raye was hit by a car while jogging. Young would be on his own on a team that was weary of his presence. He would work with two quarterbacks who, if they did their jobs and helped Young learn the system, would be out of a job.

The Bucs lost the first three games after Young arrived. Young suited up for a game at Detroit which the Bucs 'ost 30–9. Young was on the sidelines, holding a clipboard. For the first time in his life he had dressed for a football game and did not play.

As the season progressed, the Bucs continued to lose. After twelve games Bennett inserted Young into a game. But Bennett's conservative style and lack of passing protection would have ed to disaster even for Johnny Unitas. Young was not ready. But the Bucs had never been ready.

Young recalls one game at Tampa Bay that sums up his first experience in the NFL. "One time we were playing the Bears and one of our coaches looked me right in the eye and said, 'Look, Steve, I know everybody's kind of quit on you here. This is the kind of a game where you could really get hurt. Be careful out there.' I couldn't believe it. How can you enter a game thinking like that?"

DeBerg told Young that he needed exposure to some top-notch coaching before he could judge how his career would progress. In DeBerg's opinion the team that could offer such coaching was the San Francisco 49ers.

Young's two seasons with Tampa Bay felt like a prison sentence. In 1986 the Bucs started looking toward the NFL draft in which Heisman Trophy winner Vinnie Testaverde from the University of Miami would be theirs for the taking. Young requested that the Bucs trade him. In two years at Tampa Bay he had eleven touchdown passes, twenty-two interceptions, and a

82

53 percent completion rate. The Bucs granted his request and Steinberg began to shop him around the league. On April 24, 1987 Steinberg found a taker. Bill Walsh, the head coach of the San Francisco 49ers, was interested. Young soon found himself traded to the 49ers. Gillman had told Walsh that Young was the real item, the most talented quarterback he had ever seen. Gillman's word carried a lot of impact in the NFL.

Walsh had watched Young in the USFL, with Tampa Bay, and also had watched him workout in Provo in 1987 when Young was attending law school. The 49ers were looking for a backup for Joe Montana. Walsh was concerned over Montana's health. The star from Notre Dame hurt his back in the 1986 season, missed the opener, and then missed two months of play.

In Young, Walsh saw a diamond in the rough. His specialty was polishing diamonds. He had proven his specialty over and over again at Stanford, with the Oakland Raiders, the Cincinnati Bengals, and now with San Francisco.

Walsh had been a student of Sid Gillman with the Raiders. What he learned from this guru of the passing game became the foundation for everything he tried as an offensive coach. Walsh explains in his autobiography *Building a Champion,* that Gillman's influence was significant. "Sid Gillman brought refinement to the game. Every technique, every skill was isolated. There were no philosophical barriers to restrict Sid's creativity. The Raiders, under Al Davis, further developed this system."

Gillman had developed a system of offensive blocking schemes for the line. His offenses, more than other offenses of the time, freed up the tight end and running backs to be utilized in the passing schemes.

When Steve Young looks back and counts the key people in his professional career, it is no wonder the name Sid Gillman comes to the front. Gillman's influence with Walsh got Young into a system that could develop his multidimensional abilities. Putting the talent into the right system is every coach's goal. To play in a system that makes the most of his abilities is every athlete's dream.

Young would plant his feet and heart in San Francisco. The trouble was that the heart of San Francisco belonged to Montana. He was the guy who had brought the city three Super Bowls—and was soon to bring a fourth. He could walk across the bay and under the bridge without a boat or lifeline. Joe was San Francisco.

Once again Young had received a big, big break; but he also faced the fight of his life, a test that would force him to call on every strength of his character and soul.

Steinberg had earlier bought a book for Young entitled *The Quest for the Presidency, 1984*, by Peter Goldman and Tony Fuller. Inside the cover Steinberg scrawled, "Steve—One day this will be our next challenge,—Leigh." Little did Young and Steinberg realize that the challenge of playing behind Joe Montana would make a presidential campaign appear easy.

Young had handled being eighth string at BYU. He had tried to carry the USFL and the Express in Los Angeles. He'd survived Tampa Bay without injury. Now he had become the understudy to Joe.

CHAPTER
NINE

"In baiting a mouse-trap with cheese, always leave room for the mouse." —Saki

CHALLENGES

Everybody faces challenges in life. They come in many packages. Challenges are something you face up to or run away from; you handle them or bobble them. You conquer them or you let them get the best of you. Sometimes challenges cannot be conquered or overcome, but there are profits and rewards in how trials and tests are dealt with.

Such is the story of Steve Young in San Francisco. Everybody faces a Joe Montana in their lives. Steve Young just happened to face the real one. When it comes to pocket passers, Montana was the greatest who ever played the game and Steve Young was now his backup.

Steve Young's dilemma in San Francisco was simple. He did not come to San Francisco to beat out Joe Montana. Young's role was to prepare, be ready, and, if Joe could not perform like Joe, be there to somehow try to be Joe.

Whatever public and private battles were waged inside the San Francisco 49ers organization through the Montana-Young era, there is one fact which nobody takes issue with: Montana took the quarterback position to a new level.

Quarterbacks forever will be measured by the Montana standard. He was simply the best. He executed, he competed, he broke records, he won the big games. He was a master at triggering comebacks and inspired all those around him.

Steve Young is among the first to recognize Joe Montana as the master. "I played with the best to ever play the game," were Young's words during the April 1995 retirement of Montana.

You can dissect Montana's execution in the pocket into a dozen or more parts, each a lesson in itself. The parts include timing, footwork, delivery, vision, patience, courage, leadership, competitiveness, quick release, play making, decision making, reading the defensive formation, and calculating distance and velocity of delivery. In the pocket, Montana was king. He was an engineer and a concert maestro.

Montana would lead San Francisco to four Super Bowl victories. But it wasn't so much those four trophies that endeared 49er fans to him as it was his leadership on the field and that touch of wizardry that he had about him. When his team needed a clutch play, Montana made it. Time after time, season after season, Montana seemed able to deliver to his teammates and fans a last-minute drive, a backbreaking first-down sideline toss, or a blitz-beating dart to the post, resulting in victory.

Joe Montana was a hero, but not the kind Hollywood creates or TV cartoons illustrate; he was a flesh and bone superstar. And with each Super Bowl ring he delivered to teammates and the city of San Francisco, his fame grew bigger and bigger, taking on a life of its own. Montana's playmaking ability became a narcotic of sorts. People were hooked, addicted.

Montana triggered thirty-one NFL fourth-quarter come-back victories. Joe had the uncanny ability to ignite a come-back, bringing his teammates to the line of scrimmage late in a game and overpowering opponents. Kenny Stabler used to do it. John Elway occasionally does it. But Joe just plain did it, over and over again, as if the act of triggering a comeback was software and he was the Bill Gates who wrote the code. When his team appeared whipped and fans were groaning their way toward a loss, Joe produced a win. The fans celebrated as if they'd seen a miracle. In many cases, they had.

When any athlete is involved in an act as dramatic as a thrilling comeback, a last-second shot, or a herculean feat on the court or field, it pushes the hot button of fans. After all, that's why they pay the big bucks, wear the team colors, and act a little like fanatics. Montana had 49er fans in his hands and they locked Montana in their hearts. He did more than press their hot buttons. Joe had set them on fire.

Network football commentator and analyst John Madden said of Montana's quick management of pocket execution: "With most guys, it's 'I see, I step, I throw' with Montana it's 'Iseestepthrow.'"

Montana perfected the pocket performances by a quarterback. Mike Holmgren, former quarterback coach for the 49ers and head coach at Green Bay, recalls: "He had a great ability to relax and relax his teammates. In practice, he was a little bit of a jokester. Yet they knew how hard he worked at it. And when it came down to crunch time, he always came through. They saw that. He was a great leader that way, by example." When historians talk about the NFL and its great and storied quarterbacks like Johnny Unitas, Joe Namath, Fran Tarkenton, Terry Bradshaw, Joe Theismann, Roger Staubach, Dan Marino and John Elway, Joe Montana will always be the crown prince.

Bill Walsh maintains that Young's mobility and quick release are very comparable to Montana's. When he acquired Young from Tampa Bay, Walsh did so with the belief that a one-two punch of Montana and Young could confuse opposing defenses. Montana was right-handed, Young was a southpaw. Young's ability to run could disrupt a defense and Walsh liked that weapon in the 49er arsenal.

Walsh is also the first to defend Young's struggle to adapt his pocket presence to that of the masterful Montana. "So often, quarterbacks are judged on their performance with little consideration given to the level of competition or their support system from both players and coaches. That kind of mistaken judgement damaged Steve Young's reputation when he first played professionally, both in the USFL and the NFL," said Walsh.

Young, according to Walsh, had a great college career, but at the professional level his lack of fundamentals cost him when he tried to adjust to the quick and explosive play where pass rushers were stronger and faster. "The pass rush in college competition often isn't a factor," said Walsh. "Steve could take his time and throw off his back foot from anywhere on the field, and if he didn't have a receiver open, he could just run, as he possessed superb quickness and speed. But even in the USFL, pass rushers were getting closer to him, so consequently he flushed from the pocket and started scrambling and running before patterns developed downfield."

Not lost in all of this, is the fact Walsh and his subsequent coaching replacements established an offensive system that perfected the art of quarterbacking. This scheme brought five Super Bowl titles to San Francisco under Montana and Young and the hope of many more to come.

Young and Montana—a lighter moment.

The San Francisco system has proven over time that it can produce champions with different quarterbacks, running backs, receivers, and blockers. The scheme itself deserves some of the credit. Montana played in the 49er system for fourteen seasons. The quarterback has always been the focal point of that system. Rick Gosseling of the *Dallas Morning News* points out a very interesting fact about the 49er system. In five Super Bowl championships, Joe Montana and Steve Young combined to complete 109 of 157 passes for 1,487 yards and seventeen touchdowns with no interceptions. That is a quarterback rating of 135.0 in Super Bowls.

Steve Young will forever be known as the quarterback who followed Joe Montana. Although scribes and pundits will write their own accounts in years to come about Young's accomplishments, there will always be accompanying references about Joe Montana. And for good reason. Montana simply is the standard with which football fans draw a reference point.

When Montana retired from the NFL after the 1994 season with the Kansas City Chiefs, his milestones were many. He was 117–47 as a starter during regular-season games and 15–8 during playoffs. Only Fran Tarkenton (125) and Johnny Unitas (119) won more regular-season games. He was third in completions with 3,409 (Tarkenton leads with 3,686). He was fourth in attempts with 5,391 (Tarkenton leads with 6,467); fourth in touchdowns with 273, fourth in passing yards with 40,551, and third in lowest interception percentage at 2.58.

But it should also be noted that at the time of his retirement, Montana was second to Steve Young (63.65) in completion percentage at 63.24. And Montana was second to Young in quarterback rating for a career with a 92.3 rating compared to Young's rating of 96.8.

CHAPTER
TEN

"Patience is a bitter plant but it has sweet fruit." —German Proverb.

PATIENCE

Steve Young's presence in San Francisco was intended to shore up the 49ers, just in case. Quarterbacks are the highest paid players in the NFL for a good reason. With mammoth defensive linemen and linebackers moving their mass with increasingly frightening speed, quarterbacks are extremely vulnerable to injuries. After a rash of injuries benched no less than nine starters one year, the NFL changed the rules that govern when and how rushing tacklers could plow into a quarterback. The commissioner and owners reasoned that if the star quarterbacks that meant so much to NFL teams were getting creamed week after week, the overall product was getting hurt. They were right.

Montana proved to be a durable quarterback; but even the miracle maker got road miles, and the battering of the NFL took its toll on Joe. A back injury sidelined Montana for two months the year Young came to town. The next season, Montana appeared to have fully recovered but he later underwent elbow surgery. There were other aches and pains: banged-up ribs, sore hands, banged-up knees. Age also began to take its toll. Montana was five years Young's senior. From 1987 through 1990 Young managed ten starts in place of Montana while substituting as necessary when Montana started.

But Montana continued to rein. He and his close friends on the team did not easily accept the presence of Young. The 49ers were paying Young serious money; and, in the NFL coaches and owners viewed players who were payed that kind of money in a special light.

On the field, Montana faced challenges with great courage. He attacked. When he saw blitzing safeties and linemen closing in on the pocket, he'd make a step and a quick pass. He was cool under fire. If he'd fought in war, he'd have been the point man in a platoon. He was daring, courageous, and creative.

Steve Young was a challenge to Montana away from the line of scrimmage. Young was not there to be a token clipboard packer—he wanted to play. Young worked hard, he pushed, he was competitive, and he was moving in on Joe's territory. And Young was smart.

There is a story floating around the NFL that the first day Young arrived in San Francisco in 1987, he forgot his cleats. An equipment man told Young to borrow Joe Montana's. Montana wasn't due in but made a surprise visit. When they met for the first time, Young was wearing the legend's cleats, with number 16 in red ink on the back. Young backed against the wall so Montana couldn't see the number. He has been trying to fill those shoes ever since.

There was also a joke going around that number 8, (Young) would never be half the quarterback number 16 (Montana) was.

But Bill Walsh believed Sid Gillman; he believed in Young. At times through those seasons, Walsh would take Montana out of a game and insert Young. Many substitutions came when Montana was not injured. Those forced replacements by Walsh led to a mistaken belief by many 49er players and fans that Young was lobbying for more playing time behind Montana's back. That led to resentment on the team. Montana loyalists made no secret of their displeasure, however in error their perception was.

In reality, Young was just doing his job. Of course Montana started, but Young worked hard to be prepared in case the star could not play. Young wanted to play. He didn't suit up to just stand by the coach and be on TV. And Walsh was ready to give the understudy playing time.

Montana had reason to feel a little insecurity—Young was good. Also, while Montana was weak in the quote department, Young could keep reporters entertained for hours with lively story-making quips. Young was not only younger, but his legs, the magical legs, gave him a weapon that opposing defenders feared.

So there was the conflict. Montana and his miracles on one side and a hungry Young on the other. Fans were quick to take sides, and it wasn't Young who was winning. However, when San Francisco coaches dialed his number Young answered the call with success.

—1987: Young replaced Montana (hurt right hand) against New Orleans, completing four of five passes, including a 46 yard touchdown pass to Jerry Rice. Young also ran for 24 yards but suffered a concussion in the fourth quarter. Montana had a sore hamstring before the Chicago game and Young started, throwing four touchdown passes. He came in for Montana one other time that year, entering the NFC divisional playoff game against Minnesota, rushing for a team high 72 yards and a five-yard touchdown in a 36–24 loss.

—1988: Young replaced Montana (elbow injury) at New Orleans on September 4 and started against the New York Giants the following week. Young came in late in the Denver game and again started for Montana (sore back) against Minnesota. In that game, Young threw a 73-yard touchdown pass to John Taylor and scored the winning touchdown on one of the most dramatic runs in NFL history. Young scampered through almost the entire Viking defense on his way to an electrifying 49-yard score with 1:58 remaining. For his efforts Young was named the NFC Player of the Week. [The 49ers defeated Cincinnati 20–16 in the Super Bowl.]

—1989: Steve Young saw action in ten games, including three starts. More importantly, Young began coming into his own as a passer, returning to the deadly accuracy which helped him set the NCAA season and career marks in college. Young completed 64 percent of his passes (59 of 92 for 1,001 yards and eight touchdowns.) The 49ers won their second straight Super Bowl, a 55–10 win over Denver as Montana made a comeback from season long injuries. The 49ers repeat as Super Bowl Champions was their fourth—all under Montana.

—1990: Young played in six games but only started once. His agent, Leigh Steinberg, proposed that Young look elsewhere to finish his career; but Young wouldn't hear of it. He loved San Francisco and believed the 49er offense was custom-made for his abilities. He'd been to Tampa Bay, and it was a scary idea to leave Walsh's system. Although Young was beginning to catch increasing flack and scrutiny as Montana's backup, he shrugged it off and buckled up for the challenge. He was in it for the duration.

Steve Young, out of the pocket.

Steve Young checks the condition of
Joe Montana , injured in the NFC championship
game vs. the New York Giants.

Patience

The 1990 season ended with the 49ers driving for what would have been the winning touchdown against the New York Giants in the NFC championship game. A win would put the Niners in the Super Bowl for the third straight year. In the fourth quarter Montana went down with a bruised sternum and a broken bone in his right hand. Young took over. He immediately fired a 20-yard completion, getting the offense inside the Giant's 15-yard line. It appeared that Young would complete what Montana started. But seconds later all-pro running back Roger Craig took a handoff from Young and, with nobody hitting him, fumbled the football. The timing was devastating.

What could have happened? Glenn Dickey, the San Francisco *Chronicle* columnist, believes Young would have had his first Super Bowl victory as 49er quarterback. "When Roger fumbled, it was unfortunate because he was not a fumbler, that was the weird thing. If they had won that game, of course, Montana would not have been able to play the Super Bowl and Steve would have been the quarterback and I think they would have won the game and he would have gotten his career off to a much better start."

Other parts of the 49er team appeared to self-destruct after Craig's fumble. The defense couldn't stop New York from killing the clock. The Giants held on for a 15–13 win. In the next few months, Craig and All-Pro defensive back Ronnie Lott—both Montana loyalists—were traded off the team.

Then came the Steve Young era.

The next season, 1991, was Young's first opportunity to get a regular and consistent feel as the starting quarterback. Montana's injuries had taken their toll on the super star. The 49ers put Montana on injured reserve at the beginning of the season due to a tendon injury near his elbow. The move ensured that Young would be the starter for the first four games of the season. Montana did not come back the entire year. But he did not go away. The legend wandered the sidelines while Young played. This was his team, his city—and his ghost was more than a shadow.

The 49ers went ten and six in 1991 and failed to make the playoffs. Young suffered a medial collateral ligament injury on November 3 at Atlanta and missed the next five games. He was replaced by Steve Bono, who led the 4-5 team to four straight wins. Young did return and help lead the team to season-ending wins over Kansas City and Chicago. But for many 49er fans Bono's success was evidence that the open sore over the Montana-Young controversy was real. Many said: "See, even Bono is better with this offense than Young."

The fans did not start or end it. Young took criticism from the media, other teammates, and even a public lashing from Montana. Somewhere lost in the 10–6 season was the fact that Young won his first NFL passing efficiency title with a 101.8 rating. It would be the first of four passing titles for Young, an accomplishment unequalled in the game.

The 1991 season festered its way to real pain for Young. And it was not just his knee. Glenn Dickey wrote in his column that Young's bid to become Joe was failing. "Young has particular trouble with the pass in the flat. Even when he completes the pass, the receiver usually is in no position to run with the ball."

In week three of the season, CBS-TV analysts zeroed in on San Francisco's loss to Minnesota, showing how the left-handed Young appeared to not see the right side of the field. The broadcast crew kept track of how many times receivers were open on the right side and Young failed to spot them.

Later that day, the 49ers were in the Minneapolis airport on a plane waiting for takeoff. The players were strapped in their seats when the video system on board cut into a network sportscast. NBC's Will McDonough, while going over scores of the day, got to the 49er-Viking game. "I think the big thing," said McDonough, "is they [the 49ers] miss Montana. He's the guy that makes the difference in a game like this." A hush came over the team. Young sat there. He felt sick.

The next week during a radio show Jack Youngblood, a former All-Pro who was an analyst on Los Angeles' KMPC cut deep at Young. Youngblood said that the Montana replacement "will lose you more games than he'll win you."

San Francisco fans booed Young during the San Diego game. The 49ers won that game 34–14 and Young completed a season high 26 passes for a season high 348 yards. In October Young was named the NFC Player of the Month after completing 68 percent of his passes for 681 yards and five touchdowns. But it wasn't enough. Steve wasn't Joe.

The radio call-in shows were brutal to Young. That is what happens after back-to-back Super Bowls when a team loses a few games.

Young endured.

The quarterback even endured a shot from All-Pro teammate Jerry Rice, who told reporters after one loss, "I miss Joe out there." He told other reporters Young wasn't throwing to him enough. Loyalty is a tough-skinned serpent. Rice was loyal to Montana, as were many of the 49ers. It was a natural reaction. Things were not coming together as players were used to.

One problem was the 49er defense. The defense was nowhere close to the one that had played with Montana. The 49ers might be scoring points, but they were giving even more away. But in San Francisco the defense was not the issue, the absence of Joe was. Young took the fall for something that wasn't his fault. He ran out of trouble instead of holding the ball and passing, and after one game a reporter asked Rice what he thought of Young. Rice replied: "He's a great running quarterback."

But that was not all. Montana, who was relegated to street clothes on the sidelines that season, got in his verbal punches. He told the *Washington Post*: "Steve is on a big push for himself. And any time you have a competition, there is always that certain amount of animosity towards each other. I can say we have only a working relationship. That's all it is. After that, he's on my team, but as far as I'm concerned, he's part of the opposition. He wants what I have."

That comment was reported around the country. It cut deep into Young. It helped heap coals on the fire of the controversy raging in San Francisco and among 49er fans.

While Young felt the sting of knives in his back from the 49er faithful, he early on decided on a game plan and stuck by it. He would never return the words. Young knew that anything negative he said about Montana would only come back to haunt him. Besides, it was not his style. Young handled it as business—just like somebody doing a real estate deal or selling car. It was not personal, it was business.

A typical Young response to the media when questioned about Montana was this exchange with *Sport Magazine's* Mark Fainaru, more than a year later:

Fainaru: "Generally your teammates have been supportive of you. But during all this last year, there was a lot of talk about guys saying stuff."

Young: "You gotta see that it's a transition of leadership, and their loyalties were with the man that had done it with them. So you had to show that you were worthy of their loyalty, and that takes time. That's just a process, and that process was over a couple of years. And it was a challenge that I guess I chose, because I could have left a number of times. But it would be stupid to take the challenge out of trying to play well in San Francisco and take the team and be a leader on it, and then turn around and say, 'Hey, you're not treating me fair.'"

Patience

Fainaru: "What are your feelings toward Joe, beyond the fact that you always talk about the legendary status?"

Young: "I didn't realize how hyper-competitive I was until I met him. In a weird way, I understand my own competitiveness more, because, geez, that guy is relentless. He's been as successful as anyone that's ever played the game. I got to witness the personal side that could have been handled with less class; he could have been more callous. Under tremendous pressure, he was always levelheaded about everything; I admired him for that. People always want to get us at each other, and I just refused because I think I realized how competitive we are. I think away from that situation we're extremely compatible because we have a lot of things in common."

Fainaru: "But let's face it, as much as that might be true, he was not totally the picture of grace last year."

Young: "I think you have to take that in stride. I would have loved for him to have been right on the sidelines saying 'Hey, that was a great pass. This is what I would have done different. This is how I would handle it.' I mean, I would have prayed for that; that would have been the ultimate. It would have been the perfect thing for me. But it's an imperfect world. I guess over time I've learned to have a pretty good attitude."

Young was not without sympathizers, many members of the national media could see that Young was fighting a phantom in Joe's legend; that Young should be given credit for not only attacking defenses better than anybody else but packing a big burden in the process. When Montana retired after the 1994 season, Blackie Sherrod, the veteran columnist for the *Dallas Morning News,* wrote: "Sorry, but while Joe Montana may well enter history as the NFL's quarterback non pareil, some of us nitpickers can't forget the vindictive intrasquad sniping he aimed at Steve Young, when the latter succeeded him as a 49er cog. It was not Hall of Fame class. But heck, you can't have it all."

Steve Young is painfully sacked in the second quarter 1993 NFC championship game. Dallas won 30–20.

One year after that 10–6 season, Young won his second
NFL passing title with an impressive rating of 107. He was
named the league's Most Valuable Player in 1992 as well as
Player of the Year by *Sports Illustrated* and the *Sporting News*.
He was invited to the Pro Bowl. The left-hander was also given
the Eshmont Award signifying that his 49er teammates believed
him to be the team's most inspirational and courageous player.
But even that didn't totally sell in the Bay Area.

The 1992 49er season ended in the NFC championship
game at Candlestick Park against the Dallas Cowboys. Young
completed 25 of 35 passes for 313 yards and one touchdown.
But the Cowboys, led by Troy Aikman, won the game and then
went on to win the Super Bowl.

In the Bay Area, the 49er loss was generally seen as
Young's fault. MVP or not, Young blew it. The hue and cry that
echoed from Oakland to the Monterey Peninsula was that *IF*
Joe had been the quarterback he would have completed 35 of
35 and WON the game. No doubt.

That was the justice Young got from the hometown fans.

Four months later, Montana decided to make a move. If
Young was going to be the starter for the 49ers, he wanted to be
traded. To many 49er fans, that was Young's fault, too. Joe would
leave and finish his career somewhere else. Young was to blame.

The 49ers agreed to trade Joe. Then the fans cried foul.
How could this happen? Young had been told he would be the
starter and left during the off-season to finish his law degree in
Provo. The controversy over Joe's leaving continued, although
the deal went through. But, in a backhanded slap to Young, in
the closing minutes of the deal, San Francisco's front office
reversed itself and offered Montana a starting position if he
would return. Joe said no. Young was not told of the reversal
until afterwards. He was 700 miles away cramming for an exam.

What it meant for Young, explained Steinberg, was that he could never call San Francisco his team. "It meant that the words 'my team' never came from Steve's lips. I mean, it was his team, but the concept of 'my' could never come into play with him even though Steve was the quarterback. And there were a whole series of provocations where Steve just had to bite his tongue."

"The sad part," continued Steinberg, "is the fans ought to be able to hold Montana as one of the greatest who ever played the game and still appreciate Steve Young for what he does." But life doesn't work that way. Legends, whether Davey Crockett, Daniel Boone, Paul Bunyan or Joe Montana, tend to get more perfect as time ticks away.

All Young could do was play. And pass. In the decade of the 1990s, nobody did it better than the Magician from Greenwich. The 49er front office began a process of trades and player acquisitions to help build a championship team around Young. In the coming year San Francisco would put together a respectable defense to help keep opponents down while also rebuilding the offensive line to protect Young. But the weight of replacing Montana settled heavily on his mind and in his heart.

With Montana vacating the Bay Area and transplanting himself to Kansas City with the Chiefs, one would think Young had at least an even chance to win more support. And he did. Players started sticking up for him. But the ghost remained. Montana had brought the city four Super Bowls; Young had brought them none.

Tight end Brent Jones told the *Sporting News* Young was getting an unfair review: "Steve is doing things no other quarterback has ever done. But there are still people who think they can only like Joe. Steve can't please all the people in the world. There's never going to be another Joe, and Steve knows that. What more can he do? The man has a lot of class."

The 1993 season arrived with a Montana-less San Francisco team. Young remarkably repeated his 1992 feat of leading the league in passing efficiency. He became the first quarterback to ever win three consecutive passing titles. His rating was 101.2. Nobody had ever put together three consecutive seasons with ratings over 100.

Young was fast becoming the most accurate passer in NFL history—a repeat of his college career. His totals at the end of the regular season included a team record 4,023 yards. He became the first San Francisco quarterback to ever register a season with more than 4,000 yards passing. He threw 183 passes without an interception, another team record. Montana had held the previous record with 154.

The most remarkable thing about Young's 1993 season was the fact that he played the first month with a broken thumb. After missing most of the preseason, he threw three touchdown passes against Pittsburgh. Young, it appeared, had taken his position and his game to another level. He was pressing the upper limits of what any quarterback had ever accomplished with the football.

But it wasn't enough. The 49ers posted a ten and six record, made the playoffs, but lost to Dallas 38–21 in the NFC championship game. Perhaps Brent Jones was right; it would never be enough. Young went about his business; but according to friends and family, he was not himself. He couldn't relax. Always a driven person, he yearned to take on the San Francisco challenge and conquer it. He would not let it rest.

Young believed he could shake this burden—he could win, and the 49ers would win a Super Bowl with him at the helm.

"Only the educated are free."—Epictetus

VIRTUE OF LEARNING

Golf is one of those endeavors that captivates Steve Young. So was the challenge to get a law degree. Since his college days Young has worked very hard learning to play golf. He was once a partner of Johnny Miller in a nationally televised Pro-Am event when Miller took top honors. "It never ceases to amaze me about these PGA golfers and how they can do it. I can drop back, look at a defense, see all these bodies move around and throw a pass to a streaking Jerry Rice; but these guys stand still, look at a tiny white ball that is laying perfectly at rest, swing and knock it to within a few feet of where they want it 200 or 300 yards away. How do they do it?"

Something similar could be said of Young and his pursuit of a law degree. Watching and scrutinizing how Young handled the task of going to law school while juggling a football career is educational for everyone. He came, he saw, he worked, he played.

Young has been learning all his life. There hasn't been a good lesson he hasn't tried to milk for all it was worth. He has made mistakes and continues to mess some things up. But he isn't opposed to learning. Perhaps that is why Young was driven to take on law school in his spare time. If football ever failed him, he'd have something else in the game plan.

Football would not last forever. He once saw a team-mate who ended his dream of being a surgeon by breaking his hand playing football. In high school, he had a friend who broke his arm, got an infection and had to have it amputated. This guy wanted to play baseball and wouldn't give up the idea. He ultimately rigged up a cord around his stump so he could swing a bat and hit the ball. This motivation inspired Young.

Most NFL players welcome the off-season break and use it for vacations, fun, and relaxation. Young took a break, but along with the barbecues and golf came an opportunity to improve his education. He pursued a law degree. That is a tough assignment for a full-time student but Steve Young made it sort of a hobby.

Law school at best is challenging, at worst, impossible. According to law school mythology, most law schools try to get the first-year students out—out the door and out of law school. Fortunately, Steve Young has staying power and knows that the impossible just takes a little longer—in his case, twice as long, so he could fit in both football and law.

At age 32, at the prime of his professional football career, Young snagged his law degree. His Juris Doctorate is part of a future that he says will have as much to do with the court-room as it will with a playing field.

He comes from a family in which higher education and academic excellence are an expectation more than an option. The educational legacy must have seemed natural to a young man whose great-great grandfather Brigham has one of the larg-est private universities in the United States named after him. As Young prepared to graduate, he posed for photos in front of the Brigham Young statue on the Brigham Young University campus and saluted his famous ancestor.

His real legacy for advanced learning, however, came from his parents. Although his father LeGrande says he is justifiably pleased with his son's accomplishments as a superstar quarterback, nothing makes him more proud than his son's graduation from BYU's law school in 1994.

"My father says he is very happy that I am finally qualified to get a real job," said Young when he tried on his doctoral robes for graduation. "Despite what football has allowed me to do, there was never any question that a complete legal education was also in my future."

What makes Young's graduation unusual among athletes is that he tackled a rigorous program during his best playing years without waiting for retirement. To understand just how remarkable it was for Steve to gain a legal education at the same time he was preparing to make history with the San Francisco 49ers, it is helpful to take a short look at what it takes to gain a law degree.

Law students do nothing less than learn a whole new way of thinking and are cautioned not to take jobs or assume other major responsibilities. The first year of a legal education—generally considered a make-or-break time—is crammed with cum laude types about to learn how it feels to finish around the middle, instead of the top, of the class. Would-be attorneys are soon immersed in the fundamentals of contract law, criminal law, torts, legal writing, property law, and civil procedure. There are no electives and no exceptions to a prescribed course of study. The first year is considered crucial. Without sufficient legal grounding, a student is simply unprepared to pass a grueling educational process.

A trio of attorneys who do not believe they could have done what Young did, even if they had been given his incredible athletic gifts, described the challenge. "You learn a new way of writing that first year," said one. "If you arrive in the middle of the year without that training, you are coming in cold to what your classmates are about halfway through mastering."

"It is not an issue of mastering a subject; you are mastering a technique," added another.

"Perhaps I could have juggled being a superstar and a law student the second and third year, " laughed the third lawyer. "By then the courses are more fact-filled. You are studying subjects. That first year, though? No way."

If the easy route is what Young sought, he would have waited to enter law school when he could complete the program in three consecutive years. But it wasn't an easy route that got him to the top of the NFL and it wasn't an easy route that earned him his Juris Doctorate. He took the usual six semesters to finish his course work, but he did it one semester a year, a six-year process.

When his classmates entered law school in the fall of 1988, they made legal briefs and arguments while he made touchdowns. As they were learning how to think like lawyers and analyze cases, he was gaining momentum in pro sports.

So what happens when you want a solid legal education but cannot give up your day job? That was the dilemma facing Steve Young. He was exceptionally competitive, even driven, but how can you compete when you are passing a football while your 149 classmates are passing the first term?

Not only that, how do you enter the second term when your playoff season delays your entrance into the second school semester? If you are Steve Young, you haul your books, tapes, and notes with you across the country and steal moments for studying. His was an extended and rigorous game of "catch up" ball every semester he spent in law school.

"Although the professors were very supportive of me, they did not give me any special favors, nor should they have," he says. "My work load was as demanding as anyone else's."

H. Reese Hansen, dean of the J. Reuben Clark Law School at BYU where Steve attended classes, agrees. "It wouldn't have been surprising if Steve had needed additional tutoring and a great deal of help to make it through school. However, he did not consult with his professors any more often than the average student. He has a fine mind, and the intelligence that enables him to play football and other sports so well served him well through law school, too. I always had the impression he was extremely serious about his studies. He wasn't here just playing around to get a law degree. It was not a sideline. Although tough, Steve figured that sports and school were do-able at the same time."

"It also helped," Young adds, "that my football coaches and owners have been supportive, gratifying because they want your whole mind, body, and soul for the entire time you are in the leagues," he says. His teammates also cheered his efforts, and two Forty-Niners, Brent Jones and Harris Barton, flew to Utah for Young's graduation.

When asked why he didn't wait until he finished his professional career before going to graduate school, his candor was characteristically unassuming. "Law school always interested me, and, to be honest, I never thought I would succeed as a pro football player. Until my senior year at BYU, I just knew I would not make it. All of a sudden I did, but—following a couple of off-seasons—I was afraid I would be cut any moment from the football team without having the degree I wanted. I have seen too many friends fail in the attempt for a sports career. They are left with so little if they aren't educated."

For him, law school was all about hard work, dedication and self-improvement. "The discipline required for football also served me well as a student," Young explains. "Because San Francisco makes the play-offs so often, I regularly entered school after the semester had started. This made discipline vital. My motto became 'catch up and keep up.'"

Just as he had to prove himself to a throng who idolized Joe Montana—many of whom considered Steve an unwelcome interloper—he had to prove himself to a law school faculty that knows how excruciatingly difficult the curriculum can be.

The first year of law school must be taken consecutively, so Steve could not take the second semester classes when he entered law school in the winter. He simply did not have the legal background. With the encouragement of BYU President Rex E. Lee and past president Dallin Oaks—both former members of the law faculty and Lee its founding dean—Young audited a semester of law school before enrolling.

According to H. Reese Hansen, Young took the exams for his audited work and passed. This allowed him to enroll in classes the following year. "Steve not only passed, but he did very well," Hansen adds. "He was a fine law student who left school with a complete legal education. There are no qualifiers to this achievement. Other students had the benefit of the law school environment and of the time. We were all proud of him the day he graduated."

"Finishing law school is a notable achievement for anyone," Lee says. "It has been especially impressive in Steve's case because he had done it in combination with other demands. We are proud that Steve now has two degrees from BYU."

Although Young is pleased to have law school as a memory, he says it was probably good for him that he did not understand the difficulty of his juggling act. "Had I known how challenging it would be to combine law school with football, I would have taken a second look; but at times law school was my therapy," Young says. "For half my law school years, I backed up Joe Montana and was extremely frustrated about that. I

Graduation day from law school.

Steve Young. The highest profile law
school graduate since John F. Kennedy, Jr.

wasn't sure I was accomplishing anything, but when I came to school, I gained a sense of achievement."

During his tenure at BYU, Young could have easily eclipsed the other members of his class—particularly as he became more famous every year. "What you have to realize first," says Hansen, "is that Steve is an incredible person. He is really amazing. He fit in as a well-liked member of the student body. He dressed and acted like everyone else. He wore levis and was unassuming. If you did not know who he was, you wouldn't pick him out as a superstar. He did not wear a helmet to class, literally or figuratively."

An unnamed faculty member agreed, but laughed and added that the female students suddenly dressed better whenever Young, still single, joined the student body.

Associate law school dean Scott Cameron said that many professors and students thought it would be natural for Young to work in sports law. After passing the California and Utah bar exams, he could conceivably write up his own contracts or perhaps sue an overzealous linebacker for battery or he could negotiate for other players.

"I want to do something in criminal law, probably as a prosecuting attorney," Young explains. "I loved my legal negotiations classes; I was one of the reasonable men. I got a sense of adrenaline, not unlike the adrenaline I get from football. Besides, when I'm speaking before a jury, they won't throw things at me or hit me. I think that would be a lot easier."

In 1994, as he prepared to take his last set of final exams and relieved the pressure by tossing a few footballs on a university practice field, he said he felt an overwhelming sense of nostalgia. "From football through law school, BYU gave me so much. I hope I'll be able to give something back."

His law dean thinks he already has. "You can't look at Steve objectively without also looking at how his whole personality is structured around his religious faith. Steve played a football game in Atlanta in December. It was a beautiful Sunday, and that night, instead of relaxing, he gave a fireside [a spiritual talk] in the Oakland Center [church] by the Atlanta Mormon Temple. Three thousand people came to hear Steve, San Francisco 49er teammate Bart Oates, and 49er secondary coach Tom Holmoe. Every square inch was filled with people. And the spirituality of these three men showed they were 100 percent faithful to their religion. It was as fine a fireside as you would ever hear from some ideal role models. Because I know Steve, I can say with full conviction that Steve Young is an exceptional person who happens to be an exceptional football player and an exceptional lawyer."

Following Super Bowl XXIX Young appeared at a grand opening of Macy's Men's Store in San Francisco. He spent forty minutes telling stories, being funny, with self-effacing and upbeat chat. When the crowd cheered over the announcement that he had graduated from law school the previous summer, Young deadpanned: "Sure, sure. When was the last time you guys cheered a lawyer?"

*"When spider webs unite, they can tie up a
lion." — Ethiopian Proverb*

TEAMWORK

If Steve Young had one major problem in his early professional football career, it was the mistake of believing he could
make plays and carry the burden of producing wins by himself.
Although he tried hard to work his magic in the pocket, he knew
his legs could often get a first down if needed. Leaving the
pocket was often more temptation than Young could withstand.

As he settled in as the starting quarterback for the NFL's
most successful football franchise, Young began to increasingly
trust those around him. That meant sharing responsibility and
letting people do their jobs. Once Young let the team concept
work its magic, it took the pressure off his own legs and the
burden off his mission to overcome the challenge of replacing
Joe Montana.

Young simply settled down, letting the timing of a
play take its course. He would drop back and use the rhythm
of the blocking and the pass route. Then he would deliver
the ball. In time, you could put Young's moves to music; the
49er offense became a symphony. The team under Young became a fine-tuned instrument; in 1994 it developed the ultimate finesse passing game. Jerry Rice and John Taylor could

Steve Young heads for the endzone for his second touchdown run against Atlanta. Dec. 4, 1994.

attack and split any defense. Rice was establishing himself as the best receiver of all time. Before he retires, Rice will most likely catch more touchdown passes from Young than Montana. Brent Jones left the line as a tight end and forced secondaries and linebackers to worry about more than the running game or cheating on zone defenses. Rickey Watters would come out of the backfield and immediately position himself as a receiver, catching the ball and picking up crucial first-down yardage to extend scoring drives.

Young discovered that he did not have to run the football to win games, staying in the pocket paid great dividends. The burden could be carried by the many instead of the one. A sense of teamwork took over. When the front office brought in new faces, players started aligning themselves behind Young as their leader. Increasingly there were fewer veteran 49ers who had played with Joe. But the ghost did not go.

San Francisco owner Eddie DeBartolo Jr., and Carmen Policy, president, had made a commitment to rebuild the 49ers. They'd go the free agent route and use some of the most creative deal-making in the league to do it. In 1994 their work with telephone calls, brief cases, and checkbooks paid off. The 1993 draft brought the 49ers a powerful pass rusher named Dana Stubblefied from Kansas. The front office also signed free agent Tim McDonald at safety. The following year the draft added another defensive lineman, Bryant Young from Notre Dame. The 49ers were adding key players who would give Young a supporting cast to run for a Super Bowl.

Leading the list of free agents the team signed in 1994 were defensive backs Deion Sanders from Atlanta, Toi Cook from New Orleans, and defensive ends Richard Dent (Chicago) and Rickey Jackson (New Orleans). To beef up the defense with some powerful enforcers, the 49ers signed Ken Norton, a star from the two-time Super Bowl champion Dallas Cowboys and

San Diego Charger Gary Plummer. To help protect Young, they brought in his college center Bart Oates, a veteran All-Pro with the New York Jets. The 49ers signed sixteen free agents in all and most had an immediate impact.

Sanders alone gave the 49er defense a lightning-quick cover man who could take one-third of the field away from an opposing quarterback all by himself. San Francisco was loading up for some serious football.

The 1994 season arrived and so did billboards near the freeways in the Bay Area. The billboard near Highway 101 South between Fan Francisco and Santa Clara read: "Who's K.C. Playing This Week? Better Check the San Jose *Mercury News*." In other words, if San Francisco fans wanted to catch up on news about Joe and the Chiefs, there was a way. Joe was physically absent from the city, yet he was everywhere.

Steve Young couldn't miss the billboard on his way to work. Neither could he miss seeing the sea of fans wearing the number 16 (Montana's number) in Candlestick Park when the 49ers opened the season against the Los Angeles Raiders. Montana had not started a game for the 49ers in four seasons, but the legend of Joe Montana lived on.

In the opener, Young completed 19 of 32 passes for 308 yards and four touchdowns as the 49ers whipped the Raiders 34–19. Jerry Rice caught three touchdown passes and broke Jim Brown's record for career touchdown receptions.

The 1994 season was a big year for Young and it kicked off in story book fashion with the win over Oakland. The 49er front office may have paved the way for a championship with acquisitions and trades. But Young created a comfortable niche with his teammates by losing his temper during the Philadelphia game—something totally out of character.

In game five the 49ers were in Philadelphia and the Eagles were inflicting physical punishment on every San Francisco player on the roster. It was painful and it was ugly. The whipping by the Eagles would become one of the high and low points of the season for San Francisco. For Young, it was an opportunity to show his teammates that he belonged; he was one of them, and that whatever triumph or despair they could suffer, he was willing to take a number, stand in line with them.

The Eagles destroyed San Francisco 40-8 that day and were punishing an unprotected Young like crows going at naked autumn corn. It was the worst home loss in Candlestick Park in 27 years. With 4:09 left in the third quarter, the 49ers were futilely trying once again to get a first down when Eagle defensive lineman William Fuller clobbered Young so hard Young's fillings must have creaked and groaned as he collided with the ground. On the sidelines, 49er coach George Seifert had seen enough. Fuller's hit was the ninth such assault on Young and he didn't want the league's Most Valuable Player leaving the game on a stretcher. Seifert ordered backup quarterback Elvis Grbac on the field to tag Young on the shoulder as if cutting in on the dance floor.

Young, who felt like raw hamburger, was in no mood to be yanked at that particular time, at that particular place, in the middle of that specific series. The 49er's ailing offensive line was overmatched by the Eagles and they were using it to their advantage. They shut down the 49er running game, bottled up the receivers, then attacked the pocket and advanced to smother the quarterback. Young probably would have hated it just the same if he'd been replaced before that series, or after that series when both teams exchanged defensive and offensive units. Young was physically sore and emotionally sick. Around him his teammates were getting the whipping of the season, and they too were sick and tired of the Eagle's lashing on national TV. Young didn't want to abandon the cause just because it appeared hope-less. He wanted to be a partner in hopelessness if that's what everybody else who started the game was forced to gulp down.

To Seifert, it was a matter of saving Young. Grbac tapped Young on the shoulder near the huddle. Young spun around and as Ray Ratto of the San Francisco Examiner describes it: "Young whirled and shot a look at Seifert that would have dropped ev-ery roadie who ever worked for The Who." When Young came to the sidelines, he went to Seifert, and with all due respect to Seifert's rank and stripe, Young lost it, pelting the coach with a verbal barrage that turned the air blue. Young then went the rounds with quarterback coach Gary Kubiak.

The coaches were a little shocked. The 49er teammates were also shocked. Could this be the same stoic Young, Mr. Control? Even Young was sort of shocked by his actions. But on that day, on this field where Young had fought so many inner battles against ghosts, politics and himself, he wasn't going to take it without allowing his emotions to bleed freely.

"I felt like the coach was doing the right thing," said receiver Jerry Rice. "But I think the timing was a little off."

Seifert told the media after the game his decision may have been right, but his execution left much to be desired. "It was obvious I should have taken him out earlier because he took way too many shots. He took that last shot and I said: 'The hell with this. I'm taking him out.' If I didn't handle it to everyone's liking, that's because I don't have a lot of experience at this, and I hope I don't have any more."

Young told reporters he didn't know what to make of it (the yanking and the outburst). Young explained: "Today was what it was. But I'm with my guys on this deal. I don't even want to care about next week. I want today."

Kubiak explained Young hadn't been resistant when he came off the field. "He was just being competitive, that's all he was. He wants to stay in there and play. I was trying to get him to understand the situation, but in that type of situation you don't expect a player to understand. He's a 10-year pro and that's difficult. You try to be a coach and a friend and help him out."

The incident became a rallying point for the rest of the season. Young had faced terrorizing pass rushes in the early going in 1994 with little help from a banged up offensive line. Down went Harris Barton, then Steve Wallace. Jesse Sapolu followed and then Ralph Tamm joined the ranks of the injured. Young scrambled, improvised, but more importantly he help keep the 49ers on track to win a Super Bowl. And he did it without whining about how much of a beating he was taking. The entire team remembered Philadelphia and the fact Young wasn't to haughty of a quarterback to have bugged out of the game for safety of the sidelines and water cooler. Young never asked out of the assignment.

Months later Young said of the incident with Seifert: "I plead insanity. I lost my mind. When I came off the field I was frustrated mostly at the way we played and had been playing. George was saying 'You're getting rocked.' But I didn't take it that way. I was embarrassed about it. I was basically screaming to anyone who would hear me. I felt like at some point the team had to take control of itself rather than looking outside for definition, chemistry of who we are. It was like, 'Forget that. Let's just get together ourselves.' That was probably the low point and the high point of the season because we would not be the team we are unless we got humiliated like that." The public finally saw, however, what Young's teammates had known all season; that this was Steve Young's team and he belonged as the leader.

While the Philadelphia game will remain a reference point in Young's career and is sure to find a place in 49er lore, the 1994 season of teamwork and leadership would not be complete without a look at the final showdown between Young and a ghost that haunted him for a decade. The season opening win over Oakland started a myriad of plot points in the Steve Young drama. It did not take very long for a very significant story to wind its way into the script for Steve Young. And it occurred before that whipping against Philadelphia.

Game No. 2 at Kansas City would be the final Montana-Young face-off on the football field. Life would go on; glory and records would continue to rise and fall; but that Sunday in Arrowhead Stadium, to the delight of many San Francisco faithful, even if it meant their own team lost, Montana would deliver one more time.

The showdown between Steve Young and Joe Montana received top headlines throughout the country the week leading up to Sunday, September 11, 1994. Could Young shake off Joe? Could Joe get a little revenge at the expense of Young and San Francisco? Did the legend still have it?

Joe Montana, who one writer called a "demigod," was as pumped up for this showdown with his former team and Young as he had been for any game in his career. The Chiefs were a good football team and Montana, the players, and the coaches rallied around each other that Sunday to win one for Joe.

On the other side of the field, the 49ers also wanted to win one for Steve Young. But the team that took to the field in Arrowhead Stadium was not the same team that had taken apart the Raiders the previous week. Three members of Young's offensive line were out. Right tackle Harris Barton and right guard Ralph Tamm didn't play. Left guard Jesse Sapolu went out in the second quarter with a hamstring injury. The 49ers put in three inexperienced linemen to protect Young—Derrick Deese,

Harry Boatswain and Chris Dalman. That was all the more fodder for the Chiefs' outstanding pass-rush tandem of Derrick Thomas and Neil Smith to salivate over. Thomas and Smith were headhunters, two of the best abusers of quarterbacks in the league. They would come after Young and they'd go over some youngsters to do it.

Thomas sacked Young three times, and at least three other times he hit Young so hard, the fillings in his teeth must have rattled like dice in a cup. A couple of other sacks by Thomas were nullified by penalties, one of them an unnecessary roughness penalty as he smashed into Young and threw him to the ground.

Needless to say, Young took a whipping physically. The 49er's well-oiled machine was out of sync. Young couldn't do it by himself, and some of his chief soldiers were absent. Still, the Chiefs led by just one touchdown, 24–17. The 49ers had the ball late in the game, driving to tie the game, or win it with a two-point conversion. But receiver John Taylor fumbled the football with a little more than two minutes left. It wasn't Young's fault. But to the Montana-ites it *was* Young's fault—he'd failed to rally a comeback like Joe.

Montana completed 19 of 31 passes for 203 yards and two touchdowns. Young had a better percentage and more yards, completing 24 of 34 for 288 yards and one touchdown. Young did throw two interceptions; he would throw only eight more interceptions the rest of the regular season, winning his fourth NFL passing title in a row with a 112.8 rating (70.3 completion percentage).

As Montana trotted onto the field during the final exchange of possession, Young could do nothing but watch as the legend worked the clock down towards the big Kansas City win. Young's face looked like a chunk of gray granite. He had given every ounce of strength he had to win the game. He was sore,

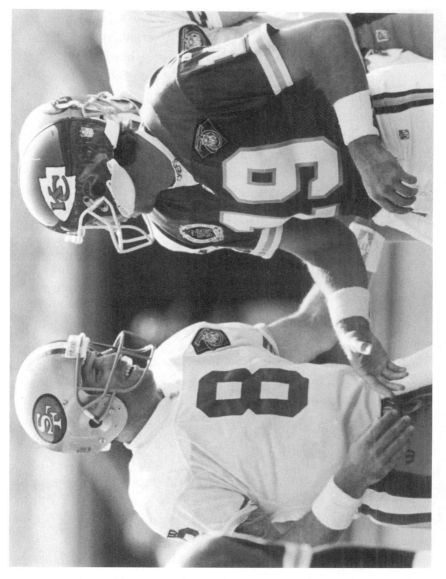

Steve Young visits with Joe Montana prior
to the San Francisco Kansas City game.

battered, tired, and frustrated. Turning from the field he hoped nobody would see as he bent over and vomited. Steve Young was empty. He had nothing more for that day, Joe's day.

Yet he did. After the gun put a period to the Major Media Event, players loosened their helmets and started towards the locker room. Young headed across the field, holding his helmet by the face guard. He walked straight for number 16 and shook his hand.

Class on the grass.

Later, in the locker room, reporters gathered around each quarterback at different ends of the stadium. Montana was asked if he could sympathize with Young as the loser. "Oh, yes, definitely. It's not an easy thing to have a game of this nature and be the guy on the short end. Just look at his passing and his winning record. He's having a great career with them. I've been on that end. I know exactly how he feels."

But Joe didn't really know how Steve Young felt. Joe didn't have to live up to Joe and beat Joe.

In the other locker room, Young stood up before the reporters, like he always does. The color had returned to his face. When asked what he thought, part of his answer was a significant gem: "The student has learned from the master."

*"I wanted my performance to speak for
itself before I spoke for it." —Steve Young*

TRIUMPH!

Olympic gold medalist Bob Richards tells the story of a writer who was working on an article about author Jack London. The writer took one of London's passages to Oakland Raider quarterback Kenny Stabler for a reaction.

Stabler, who had played at the University of Alabama in college, was a left-handed gunner on the football field and had led the Raiders to a Super Bowl. The writer wanted to get Stabler's spin on the work of London. He hoped the star quarterback would give him a good quote that could be used to start his article, so he caught Stabler and read him the following London prose: "I'd rather be ashes than dust. I'd rather my flame go out in a burning spark than to be stifled with dry rot. I'd rather be a splendid meteor, blazing across the sky, every atom in me in magnificent glow, than to be a sleepy and a permanent planet. Life is to be lived, not to exist. I shall not waste my days trying to prolong them. I will use my time."

After reading this great quote to Kenny Stabler, the writer asked the quarterback: "What does this mean to you?"

Stabler pondered the question for a few seconds. Then he answered: "Throw deep."

Steve Young preparing to throw deep

Triumph!

Young's college coach, LaVell Edwards, loves to tell this story of Stabler and the Jack London quote. He often uses it to set up commentary about his own left-handed All-American, Steve Young. "It all comes down to how you look at things, at life and how you approach it. Steve always approached things with the attitude that he could be successful," says Edwards.

Steve Young's first Super Bowl could be called a Ken Stabler reaction to the London quote: Young went deep and he made some people pay for his time.

San Francisco is a city that handled a gold rush, triumphantly arose from the rubble of earthquakes, and has an NFL franchise that has won more Super Bowls than any other. Super Bowl XXIX may hold a particular light for the city, mainly because of the effort by the entire Forty-Niner organization to bring the trophy back home, but also because this Super Bowl was Steve Young's first and it left an impression. "Steve had two great years," said 49er coach George Seifert. "But this season he took it to another level. He was the equal to anyone who has ever played quarterback for the 49ers. Joe set some high standards for this club. But there were games this year when Steve matched those standards."

The whole event is also memorable because it lasted more than two weeks in TV highlight replays, beginning with the NFC championship game with Dallas where Steve Young finally smiled a Grand Canyon smile.

The Cowboys and 49ers were fighting for more than the right to go to the Super Bowl. They were fighting for the label of the NFL Team of the 90s. The 49ers were the rebuilt machine keyed by an offense George Lucas and Stephen Spielberg might have invented. The Cowboys had the league's toughest defense and were a two-time Super Bowl champion. Something had to give. Initially it was the ground. The turf in Candlestick Park in San Francisco was a spongy, muddy quagmire, a mud-pot brought on by a month of above-normal rainfall. With thirty-four counties receiving flood waters, California was a federal disaster area.

The media hyped this NFC championship game as the actual Super Bowl. The winner could be crowned right then and there. Period. To heck with Miami two weeks later, this was for all the marbles, a battle between the league's two titans. And no love was lost in the process. A fight broke out while the two teams came out for warm ups. Once civility was restored, the 49ers jumped to a 21–0 lead, taking advantage of three Dallas turnovers and a hobbling star running back Emmitt Smith.

Young and company were keyed up: each time Dallas stumbled, there were the 49ers, ready to pounce. Cowboy coach Barry Switzer received a lot of the criticism for the way this game played out. As the game ended he was penalized for bumping an official while protesting a no call. Just before halftime, down 24–14, the Cowboys had the ball with just over a minute to play and the entire field before them. Switzer failed to run down the clock and get the Cowboys regrouped. Instead, Dallas ran three quick pass plays—all incomplete—and then punted to the 49ers. John Jett's punt was a fell way short on the soggy field, and the 49ers downed the ball at the Dallas 39.

Giving the 49er offense the ball inside midfield with a few seconds left is like swimming the shark-infested Great Barrier Reef wearing a bloody sirloin steak as a ballast. Young dropped back and noticed the Cowboys had dropped into man coverage on Jerry Rice. He fired a timing strike to the corner of the end zone and Rice blasted down the field and squared out his pattern to the corner pylon. Young threw the pass just as Rice made his cut and the league's best receiver sprinted out of the coverage and hauled in the touchdown pass. Young was 13 of 29 on the day for 155 yards. But two of the passes were for touchdowns and he ran for a third.

At the conclusion of the game, Young celebrated in a way he had never done before. He let himself go emotionally and ran around the field to the cheers of the home crowd. As he looked into the stands with a wide smile, fans gathered up clumps of soggy sod as souvenirs.

Young had gone deep and was now in his first Super Bowl.

"I've come to grips with the chip on my shoulder," Young told reporters. "There have been a lot of hurdles, a lot of hoops to jump through. It's like I've been chasing after a rabbit at a dog track."

One of his best friends from college, Jim Herrmann, was in the stadium and told reporters few knew the burden Young had carried with him through the years, working in the shadow of Montana. "Those were tough years. Every time I talked to Steve or saw him in the off-season, it seemed that Montana was constantly on his mind. He had to submerge his personality. He couldn't be himself around the team because anything he said or did could be interpreted as a challenge to Joe. It got to a point where people in the clubhouse were judged on the basis of whether they went over and talked to Steve."

Few TV watchers escaped the outpouring of emotion when Young took the 49ers to the Super Bowl by walking over the bodies of the Cowboys that Sunday. When Young celebrated on the field, he broke out of an emotional prison that had kept him bound for nearly a decade.

The Super Bowl on January 29, 1995, was anticlimactic to that NFC title game win over Dallas. In fact, it was a sorry excuse for a Super Bowl. The 49ers abused the AFC champion San Diego Chargers, and, if it hadn't taken place as a sporting event, it would have been a felony. Even the oddsmakers gave the 49ers more than three touchdowns before kickoff.

Young and the 49er offense hit the Chargers quick and deep, striking twice on touchdown passes of 44 yards to Jerry Rice and 51 yards to Rickey Watters in the opening minutes. Before the 49–26 blowout was finished Young threw a Super Bowl record six touchdowns. He completed 24 of 36 passes for 349 yards and no interceptions. Surprisingly, he was also the game's leading rusher with 49 yards.

The performance of Young and the 49er offense prompted longtime NFL analyst and former coach Hank Stram to state that Young was on his way to becoming one of the game's greatest quarterbacks. "This is the best-looking offense I've seen in all my years I've been involved with the NFL. Young can turn defenses upside-down with his running."

The Super Bowl completed a San Francisco playoff run under Young which produced 131 points—the most playoff points by an offense in NFL history. San Francisco coach George Seifert told reporters afterwards that Young had risen to the level of Joe Montana.

For Young, the Super Bowl ring meant much more than the statistics. The victory opened a new era in his life. No longer could people criticize him for failing to take the team to a Super Bowl. And win. This was Young's first time on the Super Bowl stage and he delivered in a big, big way. In the celebration that followed the Young-49er triumph, Deion Sanders called Young, "truly the best who has ever played."

Young tried to avoid mentioning the M-O-N-T-A-N-A, word afterwards. Instead, there was a lot of talk about getting the monkey off his back. "Honestly, I have distanced myself from it all [comparisons to Montana]. I did so a couple of years ago. I want my performance to stand for myself and my team-mates. It does a disservice to the team when it's talked about that way. I understand it, but there will be a time when I think [the media] will appreciate the distance [I kept] from whatever else happened in San Francisco.

"It was difficult to face it, and some days I wasn't sure I was doing very good. You know the standards I had to live up to. That's why this is one of the most precious times in life to finally get there. Critics? To hell with them. Go to someone else for a change."

All season long Harris Barton would symbolically take the monkey off Young's back at every significant 49er game, according to San Francisco columnist Glenn Dickey. So it was fitting that in the closing minutes of the Super Bowl rout over San Diego, Barton came over to Young on the sidelines and pretended to take the monkey off his back. The scene was captured by network television and became part of the 1994 season and the Steve Young saga.

Following the victory Young was the complete center of attention, from his circling of the field to celebration on the sidelines with teammates. The chimp was heavy and now Young was light. He owned the pocket. He had just completed the best game of his life. That it took place in the Super Bowl was all the more exhilarating. Barton turned to Young and told him to remember the moment. "I looked at the scoreboard and watched the people. I took myself out of the emotion, and I was the observer."

Young was given the championship trophy in ceremonies afterwards. He kissed it. He held it tight. He wouldn't let it go. "There was just so much emotion poured into that one little object."

For Young that trophy was symbolic; it represented the conquering of almost every wind that had blown against him. He had triumphed over more than most will ever know. NFL officials handed him the keys to a Buick Riviera, a prize given to the games Most Valuable Player. Young told reporters he wouldn't know what to do with it unless he scratched it a few times so it would seem like his own. A month after the game he traded it for a 4X4 pickup.

That night lasted a very long time for Young. There were celebration parties after the interviews and showers. There were teammates, friends, family and a long walk home from Joe Robbie Stadium. When Young's chartered limo encountered gridlock in Fort Lauderdale, he opened the door and started to walk down the sidewalk towards the San Francisco 49er's hotel. He wore denim and plaid. With his hair matted down, a limp and a big smile, he made his way to the hotel security gate where the guard asked if he had any passes.

"Yeah, I threw six of them."

As tradition in big sporting events dictates, star athletes are approached before games and contests and asked by Disneyland to make a commercial. When asked at the scene of victory what they will do next, the star is supposed to say he is going to Disneyland. Young was approached by Disneyland's advertising agency before the game and asked to do a commercial if the 49ers won the Super Bowl. Young refused, unless, he explained, teammate Jerry Rice could go with him and they both do the commercial together after the victory. They did. It was kind of a turn of specter for Rice, the greatest receiver of all time. Just a few years ago during the Montana-Young controversy, he did the politically correct thing when Montana was starting, calling Young a very good running quarterback. Now, after Super Bowl XXIX Rice, who needs no set up lines from anyone for his prowess and stardom, accepted a setup from Steve Young.

Surmized Young of the Disneyland gig with Rice: "I try to involve everyone. If it's foolish, then I only look half foolish. If it's great, then it's 50 percent great for someone else."

Did Young shake off the monkey and bury it deep? Only time will tell. But in the wake of the 49er's fifth Super Bowl victory—this time by Young—there are some achievements by the 49ers which loomed significant in 1994-95.

—In four years as the starting San Francisco quarterback, Young won an unprecedented four consecutive NFL passing titles. Only Johnny Unitas (1964 and 1967) and Joe Montana (1989 and 1990) have won passing titles more than once in their careers.

—Steve Young's 1994 passing rating of 112.8 ranks as the best single-season effort by a quarterback in NFL history.

—The 35 touchdown passes thrown by Young in 1994 rank as a team record, surpassing 31 by Joe Montana in 1987.

—The 70.3 percent completion rate by Young in the 1994 season is a new team record, topping Montana's mark of 70.2 percent in 1989.

—Heading into the 1995 season, Steve Young is the most accurate college and NFL quarterback to ever play the game. His 96.7 career passing rating is the NFL's best mark ever, surpassing Joe Montana's career rating of 92.2. Young is also the NFL's new active leader in completion percentage, with a mark of 63.64 percent, bettering Dallas' Troy Aikman's mark of 62.43 percent.

—The 1994 San Francisco team ranks as the most successful offense in club history. The offense established team marks for most points in a season (505), most touchdowns (66), and average points per game (31.6).

"When Joe Montana ran this offense," said offensive lineman Harris Barton, "it was like he was conducting a symphony. "When Steve Young runs this offense, it's kind of like a jam session. They both produce great music, but just a little different."

137

"Every man is entitled to be valued by his best moment." —Emerson

THE ESSENCE OF COMPETITION

Offensive tackle Harris Barton rented a room in his house to Steve Young during his early days with the San Francisco 49ers. "Late in the season," remembers Barton, "I went into his room to steal a pair of socks. I looked in the drawer and found thirteen uncashed paychecks. I asked him about them and he said: 'I haven't done anything to earn them. So I'm not going to cash them until I do.' They told me he wasn't a finance major in college," Barton added.

Television producer Mike Hemingway remembers a similar Young story. The time frame was soon after Young signed his $40 million deal with the Los Angeles Express. During the off-season Young joined the KBYU television crew as a color commentator for the Brigham Young Cougar broadcasts.

One weekend when BYU played at the University of Hawaii in Honolulu, Hemingway waited for an overdue Young to show up for the flight. Young had apparently slept in while napping on the floor of Gordon Hudson's apartment. Young, hurrying to make the flight, grabbed a gym bag and threw in some clothes. "He didn't pack anything hardly at all," says Hemingway.

Young got on the plane and Hemingway made his way to Young's seat a little embarrassed. Hemingway had seventy-five dollars to give Young. It was his $25 per diem for the three-day trip to Honolulu. Hemingway felt his face blush as he approached the young millionaire and gave him the money.

"Sorry it isn't that much, but here's your per diem money for the trip," said Hemingway.

"Geez, thanks Mike," said Young, his face lighting up. "Would you believe it? I forgot my wallet, I was in such a hurry to leave. I was hoping to bum some money off the football team to get by."

Amazing, thought Hemingway. Amazing.

But these are vintage examples of Young. It never has been about money. When it came to the green stuff, he could care less. Throughout his life, Steve Young has been a driven man, a motivated athlete. He always strived to leave no stone unturned to succeed and win. But it was never about money.

One summer, soon after he was named the San Francisco starter, Young, a movie buff, decided his favorite current offering in the cinemas was *Searching for Bobby Fischer*, the story of a 7-year-old chess prodigy. Young told *People Weekly* magazine in 1993 that he liked the show over *The Fugitive*, and *In the Line of Fire*. Said Young of the Fischer character: "They're trying to [teach him to] become a champion by having contempt for his opponents, but he can't do it. I wish parents would understand that if their child drops eight fly balls one day, then only drops six the next, that's a reason to go to Dairy Queen. The principal [thing is] competing against yourself. It's about self-improvement, about being better than you were the day before."

Certainly Young's moment of triumph during Super Bowl XXIX, the raised arms, the big grin, the circling of Joe Robbie Stadium after the win over the Chargers, captures a picture of Young and his quest to bring the 49ers a fifth Super Bowl. But another enduring moment in the Young saga will stick in the minds of many NFL fans forever: "The Run" against Minnesota in 1988. Analyst John Madden joins other football experts in labeling The Run one of the NFL's most dramatic plays. In retrospect, The Run epitomizes Steve Young's story.

Young's ability to run has become legendary in the NFL, mainly because high-paid quarterbacks just do not often do it. And when they do, they like to slide on the ground to avoid getting hurt. Young does his share of sliding too, by edict of coaches, but he also runs to win. And that makes him dangerous for opponents.

Said Atlanta Falcon defensive end Tim Green: "On Sunday morning when you have to play Young, you wake up with a sickening feeling and a headache. I can honestly say those are the only times I've ever approached a game conceding that an opposing player's going to make big plays no matter what we do."

The Run took place Oct. 30, 1988 against the Minnesota Vikings in Candlestick Park in San Francisco. Joe Montana was injured and Young was making another of his scattered starts. Young was not fully adjusted to piloting the offense and at times played harried in the pocket. As always, he relied on his feet to get him out of a bind on the field. Those feet rarely betrayed him.

The 49ers were losing the game and were on the verge of dropping to 5–3, further behind the Los Angeles Rams and New Orleans Saints in the conference standings. San Francisco fell behind 7–3 and had managed just four first downs in the first half. Young was sacked four times and had just forty yards passing by halftime. But after halftime, the 49ers shifted to some play-action sets with Young faking handoffs, pulling up and throwing for first-down yardage instead of long launches. Young threw for 152 second half yards, including a 73-yard touchdown to John Taylor.

But the Viking defense was getting to Young. On that touchdown pass to Taylor, Young was smothered and never saw the catch or score. "A couple of times I think we literally almost killed him," said Viking rusher Al "Bubba" Baker.

The Vikings took a four-point lead (21–17) into the final four minutes of the game. With the game slipping away from Bill Walsh's 49ers and the offense stalled at midfield, the day looked bleak. The Vikings appeared to have the momentum, the 49ers, and Young.

With just over one minute left in the game, it was third down and four. The 49er play called for Young to run a "Double Underneath," in which the two inside receivers in San Francisco's formation would break to the outside while the two wideouts would drag across the inside. Young dropped back to pass near his own 40 yard line. The play broke down and Viking rushers zeroed in on Young.

Young was looking for Mike Wilson when Viking quarterback killer Chris Doberman raised his hands up, blocking Young's vision downfield. Young moved to the side, looking for a passing lane to throw through. Spinning away from Doberman, Young looked for tight end Brent Jones who was supposed to come down the field, pull up and stop right in the middle. Young needed only a couple of yards for a first down to keep the drive alive so, as usual, he thought he could take off and get the necessary distance.

In a quick burst of speed, Young stepped out of a tackle at the line of scrimmage and then pivoted towards the east sideline as recovering Viking linebackers and defensive backs broke

142

off coverage and tried to run him out of bounds. At that instant, Young cut back, veering out of diving tackles by bewildered defenders. Young was going to just run out of bounds and take the first down until he saw running back Tom Rathman make a block. Cutting behind Rathman's interference, Young picked up another block from Jerry Rice on Viking linebacker Jesse Solomon and headed back towards the middle of the field.

Carl Lee grabbed Young's jersey, but the quarterback broke free. He cut in front of Viking defenders Brad Edwards and Cris Martin, leaving them clutching air. Young's outstanding 4.4 speed is quite phenomenal for a quarterback in the NFL. When the Magician stresses out his cleats, anything can happen. It happened that day.

"I just think Young saw an opportunity and his athletic ability allowed him to do it," said Baker. "This is no discredit to Joe, but I don't thing Joe could have made that run. He would have probably slid 10 or 15 yards down the field. Steve really wanted it."

Young later said he was going to stiff-arm Solomon until Rice took out the big tackler. Young broke free and there were no remaining Minnesota players to prevent a score. Young, his legs pumping as he tried to catch his balance, stumbling and almost tripped at the eight-yard line. Somehow he regained his balance and like a drunken man, lunged over the goal line. A TV shot panned to the 49er bench and there Joe Montana was seen laughing, not at Young but at how the play made the Vikings look like the Key Stone Cops. The play electrified the crowd and the stadium rocked as if hit by lightning. Even the 49er faithful, used to seeing great plays, were awestruck. Young had made the Vikings look like a high school defense.

"I was kind of laughing because I couldn't believe I was falling into the end zone," Young told reporters later. It was kind of embarrassing. I was thinking I was going to go down

Steve Young in the classic pose that strikes fear
into the hearts of NFL defenses.

about the three, and that would have been embarrassing." Young, winded and his strength expended, got up with the help of his teammates. He was too spent to dish out any high fives.

"That was natural God-given talent," said teammate Roger Craig. "He just went out there and won the game. You know, he won the game."

Walsh called Young's move "an unbelievable athletic feat." It also helped that Young's timing couldn't have been better. Walsh got a 24–21 win. The 49ers improved to 6–3 and would go on to beat Miami in Super Bowl XXIII.

The Run was vintage Young. He saw an opening, improvised, and then just performed. "It was inspirational," said Craig. Baker said that it was a case of one man's will to win. "It wasn't like we let him do it. It was a great play. Games are won and lost on great plays."

In the media assault on Young that followed that October win, somebody asked Young if his run compared to the spectacular and dramatic pinch-hit home run by Kirk Gibson in the 1988 World Series that fall.

"No," said Young, "because he got to trot."

Steve Young is one guy whose style is not to go trotting when a good heady run will do. His life has never been about money. Nor has it really been about being accepted, wrongly judged, or even replacing Joe. Life, says Young, is about self-improvement—becoming better than you were the day before. It is reason to go to Dairy Queen.

Pictures

152

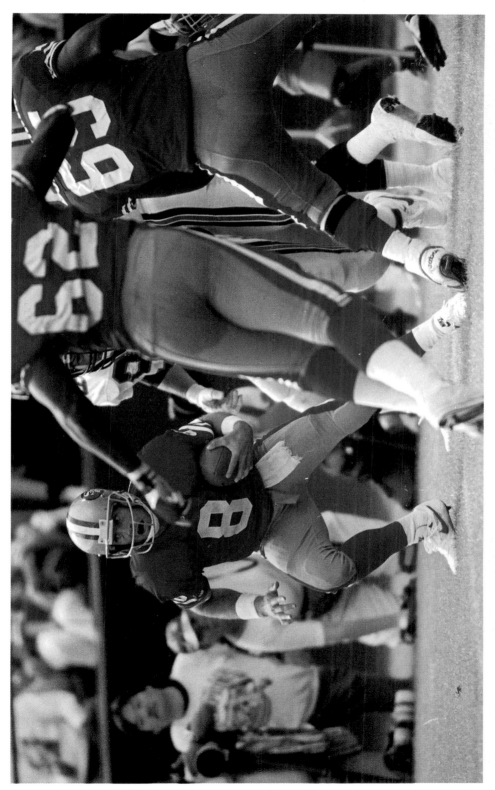

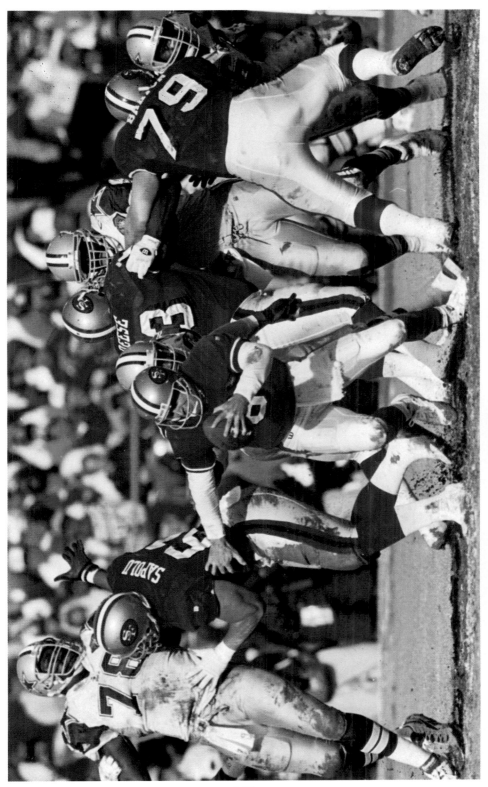

*"Whatever limits us, we call
Fate."—Emerson*

AMONG THE BEST

How good of a quarterback is Steve Young?

That question is kind of like asking who bakes the best pie? Or what is the best car to buy? Is Emmitt Smith a better runner than O.J. Simpson? People have their preferences, Steve Young has both his staunch followers and his serious critics.

Young may inspire some, but he upsets others. There are those who take his statistics and records to prove a point that he belongs in the Hall of Fame someday. Others argue that he is the product of great systems in college and the NFL, nothing more and nothing less. Some count Super Bowl victories as a measurement of success. Others claim that to rate a quarterback through victories or Super Bowls is unfair because QBs need great teammates to make a winning team. A quarterback's success certainly depends on a supporting cast. Some quarterbacks don't even call their own plays but are captives of the ego and intelligence of the coach in the press box. There are those who will blame a quarterback for any loss and give total credit to a quarterback for a win. Still, in the study of quarterbacking, there are many gauges to look at including physical skills, arm strength, delivery, accuracy, range, leadership, courage, intu-

Steve Young playing with the best in the
1993 Pro Bowl in Honolulu, Hawaii.

ition, field vision, scrambling ability, injury avoidance, and playmaking ability. But it is still usually pure opinion as to who does it best.

The book is still open on Steve Young and his four consecutive passing titles. Nobody can really put a final label on him until he retires and the statistics, film replays and records speaks for him. In the meantime, debate continues, opinions flourish.

In San Francisco, his teammates are quick to offer their praise. In Dallas, Miami, and Denver there are plenty who argue that Troy Aikman, Dan Marino, and John Elway are supreme. All are entitled to their opinions. Football is entertainment, it is not an objective science.

Glenn Dickey, sports columnist since 1971 for the *San Francisco Chronicle* has covered the 49ers extensively and is working on a book about the team's history. Dickey says Young is generally well-liked by 49er fans. "Although there is still a small group of Montana people that are never going to accept him because Montana can't be replaced in their minds, that group has shrunk enormously in the last couple of years."

One place where the debate over who is the best quarterback in the NFL flourishes is on the internet, a worldwide forum linking computer owners who have access and a mind to type messages into a newsgroup. Football fans are a big part of the internet and one newsgroup in particular is dedicated to the 49ers. (The newsgroup access code is alt sports.football.prc.sf-49ers). On this frontier Young is dissected along with other NFL quarterbacks. Here is a sampling of internet postings on the subject.

Mike Ammerman at New Mexico State University ranks the quarterbacks as follows:

1. Dan Marino: best passer and thinker ever.
2. Steve Young: best athlete and a great passer.

3. Drew Bledsoe: great arm, too many interceptions.
4. John Elway: thinks, throws and a great leader.
5. Warren Moon: new system, and still played great.
6. Troy Aikman: great cast, but someone has to get the ball there and he does it as well as anyone.
7. Randall Cunningham: great athlete, panics under pressure sometimes.
8. Brett Favre: good arm, good athlete, no brains.
9. Jeff George: strongest arm, needs more quality experience.
10. Rick Mirer: could be. . . . I couldn't think of anyone else above average.

Writes Kyle Nichols: "The best QB in the game today HAS to be Drew Bledsoe. Young, Marino and Acheman [Aikman] have a great supporting cast to compliment them. Bledsoe on the other hand has taken no-names and made them household names. His arm and accuracy are second to none, and in a year his judgment will be too."

Writes David Poland: "Truth be told, if there was a draft with Montana, Marino, Elway, Kelly, and Young, Young would probably be my fifth pick. Of course, Young will probably be around longer than the others and will still be great, but he's not a guy who's name will ever be whispered among the greats fifteen or twenty years from now. Except by Niner fans who think Derek Loville can replace Ricky Watters."

Responds Marvin Ruth to Dave Poland: "Anyone read *Sports Illustrated*? The above statement would be great for the 'This Week's Sign That the Apocalypse is Upon Us' section. I don't think I've seen much more idiotic comments posted to this group since I had access to it. He would rather take Kelly and Elway? Elway is a cocky, arrogant jerk who will never lead his team to anything. And Kelly, although very good for some time, is now plummeting rapidly. He must throw two times as many interceptions as Young. In fifteen to twenty years from now, people WILL talk about Young on how he won 'four' quarterback titles in a row..., and of course how Kelly lost 'four' Super Bowls in a row and how Elway lost 'four' Superbowls. Just my thoughts."

From another cyber pilot, unnamed: "I think currently [the best] is Young and then Favre and Marino are all about the same. I would take Young on his scrambling ability though, and his toughness. I don't see how anyone could ever doubt him not giving his all. Aikman needs to be the Aikman of old to be on this list."

The discussion turns to statistics. Here one internet surfer makes a chart comparing Young, Montana, Marino, and Dan Fouts:

	Young	Marino	Montana	Fouts
5,000 yard seasons	0	1	0	0
4,000 yard seasons	1	6	0	3
3,000 yard seasons	3	10	8	6
Seasons under 1000	4	2	2	1
Seasons of 40+ TDs	0	2	0	0
Seasons of 30+ TDs	1	4	1	2
Seasons of 20+ TDs	3	11	6	6
Seasons under 10 TDs	6	1	3	4

Note how Young is dead last in every category except for 4,000 yard seasons, where he is third, and 30-plus TD passes, where he is tied for last?

A response follows: "These numbers compare nothing. Did you count Young's years as a backup? Yes. Now that really isn't fair. Are you saying he's not as good of a quarterback because he was on the same team with the best quarterback ever? Besides, those stats are Marino's best attributes. Compare quarterback ratings or completion percentage. You picked Marino's best abilities and used those to measure who's the best. That would be like rating a quarterback on rushing, scrambling ability. It's not a fair chart you have there."

Another chips in: "Hey, what's up? First time caller. Just noticed your discussion about the best quarterbacks today. There is no question Steve Young is the best quarterback in the game today. No one has accomplished more while going through so much. He has absorbed tremendous amounts of criticism from fans and the media. Yet he continues to win passing titles and maintain his cool under fire. This past season was the icing on the cake. Yes, he does tend to throw high over the middle and does not lead receivers out as well as Joe. But then again, there will never be another Joe. As for Marino, or Favre, or any of the other guys, they'll need to take a back seat."

The discussion will go on and on as long as there are games to be played.

Glenn Dickey says statistics need to be taken for what they are worth and any statistical achievement like Young's four NFL passing titles in a row is noteworthy. "I think he has definitely improved as a quarterback and even as a passer. The two have gone hand in hand. He's learned to make better decisions on whether he should pass, whether he should run, where he should throw. He's said himself that a quarterback in the 49er system should always complete at least 60 percent of his passes, because the way the system is set up. And if you look at not just Steve and Montana, but even lesser players, like Jeff Kemp played for one year there when Montana was out for back surgery and he's never done anything anywhere else. Steve Bono played well with the 49ers and he has not done anything anywhere else to make people think he was that good of a quarterback. Matt Cavenaugh was a good backup and failed when he went elsewhere."

"The system itself is a great one of quarterbacks, and of course, he's had great people to throw to too. So to say that because he has the highest rating means that he is the best of all time would be a stretch, but obviously it's a combination of things. But it's a great achievement for him."

Dickey co-authored a book with Bill Walsh and, as a friend, he lobbied for Walsh to get Young from Tampa Bay. "I campaigned to get him traded—for the 49ers to get him in a trade—because I knew that the situation in Tampa Bay was not working out for him. I saw him play in the USFL and I thought he had tremendous talent. Walsh is a guy who has independent judgments, he doesn't wait for somebody else to tell him a guy's good. At the time the feeling around the league was that he [Young] would never make it, but I knew that he would if he got here and Bill could work with him, and he did. Steve will tell you that is the biggest factor in his becoming a really good quarterback as opposed to just a great talent who was playing quarterback."

According to expert observers, Young may have a ways to go before his career can be compared to those of Montana, Bradshaw, Staubach, Unitas and Marino. But his performance in his first Super Bowl year is among the best of all time. The 1994 performance by Young which brought the record 112.8 quarterback rating was about as good as a quarterback could perform, claims Dickey. "And that stacks up very well to anything Montana ever did or any of the great quarterbacks of the past. When you're ranking a quarterback on a career, he needs a few more of those years. I think he'll get them. I've written that

I think he'll be in the Hall of Fame. So he wouldn't be off this, because it's too short a time, even though he's been great in that period. But I think he's capable, he's in very good shape. He's capable of playing four or five more years at this level. That would rank him with the best of all time. He's on his way to earning it. It's too short a career for now, not through any fault of his; he was capable of playing much earlier."

Dickey said he observed key elements in Young's game early on and those observations have held true and are being lived out in his career. "No. 1, I knew he could really throw the ball. Everyone focused on his running ability, which was a plus, but from his college years when he was completing 70 percent of his passes, you don't put up those kinds of figures if you can't really throw the ball. I could see in the limited times he played, he could throw some passes. He was always a much better long passer than Montana. He threw some passes early on to Jerry Rice that were really beautiful to watch. I could see the talent there. As intelligent as he is, I knew he could pick up the system here."

" I thought it was a question of time and getting a chance to play. One thing I thought other writers didn't understand was that when he did get in when Montana was the quarterback, and Steve did get a chance to play, it was usually in special circumstances where he was supposed to go in and make a brilliant individual play."

Dickey says Walsh put Young in against Denver at Candlestick Park where the wind was blowing so hard you could hardly throw the ball. But Walsh figured Steve could probably run and be effective that way. Another game Walsh put in Young in place of Montana was against the Bears at Wrigley Field when it was cold and the Bears' defense had rendered Montana ineffective. "Walsh thought Steve could buy some time with his feet and get the pass off. But he was always being asked to do something out of the ordinary; he wasn't given the chance to play the game and settle in like a quarterback normally would. So when he got a chance I think he definitely proved he could do it."

As the years passed, and Montana left San Francisco and many of his loyal teammates were traded or retired, Young slowly began to win over his teammates. The 1994 season marked a significant blending of Young with other players. In that process Young came out of his shell, so to speak. Young played like Steve Young could and allowed himself to be more himself. The result was a chemistry that successful teams have to have in order to win. Said Dickey, "When Montana was around, Young was always concerned about saying anything that might be interpreted the wrong way."

So, for Young watchers, is Young finally Young? And if he won four consecutive passing titles not really being himself, what lies in store for the 49ers in the future?

*"What a man does in his spare time defines
who he really is." —Unknown*

OFF THE FIELD, OFF THE RECORD

Steve Young Day on the Navajo Indian Reservation is not big on ceremony. When the National Football League's Most Valuable Player shows up in Blanding, Shiprock, Window Rock, or Tuba City there are no television cameras. Nobody calls a press conference for a photo shoot. The word goes out on wings of the wind and Indian schoolchildren gather from the desert mesas and juniper covered buttes. They flock to town and fill football stadiums to embrace their hero, a handsome, athletic American icon.

The Navajo Indians are the nation's largest Native American tribe. On Steve Young Day the hearts of these impoverished people forget a life of poverty and despair. Few Navajo families have escaped the ravages of alcoholism and high mortality. Corruption has rocked their tribal leadership, a familiar disappointment. Desperate health conditions, low employment and low income combine with rampant child abuse to mark the Navajo existence. Few Americans know anything about these problems. Or care.

The Navajos have adopted Young's San Francisco 49ers as the official NFL team of the tribe. Syndicated 49er play-by-play radio broadcasts blare from KTNN in Window Rock. Games are heard all over the Indian nation from Blanding, Utah to Tuba City, Arizona. The tribe knows Young. He gives them a diversion. He gives them hope.

The spring ritual of Steve Young's appearance among the Navajos is part of Young's effort to provide educational scholarships for students. The link is a result of Young responding to a request from American Indian Services Director Dale Tingey. Young could have just mailed in the money. But his appearances speak volumes as he quietly treks to the reservation during the off season and speaks to the youth and their leaders.

Young's message to the Indians is simple. Life is worth a fight. Nobody but you should define what and who you are or what you can do. Having heroes and setting goals are important. And never lose sight of the horizon where tomorrow starts at the ending of today.

On the surface, Young and the Navajos have almost nothing in common. Young comes from a modest section of affluent Greenwich, Connecticut. He is the son of a corporate lawyer. He is one of the NFL's highest paid players supplemented by additional lucrative endorsements piling in after his MVP performance in Super Bowl XXIX. He is a law school graduate. He is on the threshold of becoming the most accurate and productive NFL quarterback of all time. Success slides off Young like dew off a sandstone arch.

The Navajo people are poor. Per capita income is less than $5,000 a year. Approximately 70 percent of Navajo homes are still without electricity. In some end-of-the-road settlements on the reservation, families live in clay-and-log hogans facing the rising sun. Some do not speak English. There is an alarming 70 percent dropout rate among the Navajo youth; the tribe's hope for tomorrow.

But, as the Navajo have fought their demons in real life, battling serious challenges in a way Young could never know, he has trudged along his own challenging path. Since leaving BYU in 1985 Young has traveled a road in the USFL and NFL that would bring lesser men to their knees. His triumph in Super Bowl XXIX was celebrated by Americans as a classic mastery of conflict. Young won where others would have crumbled. He exalted himself with his teammates in 1995 when others would have quit. And Young remains untainted by greed, drugs, and other indulgences that are becoming the ruination of sports.

The year America lost Major League baseball in a battle over money and power, Young got his Super Bowl ring and a law degree. He cast off the ghost of Joe Montana. And the Navajos got their hero, a man who spoke of dreams and then lived them.

Steve Young Day on the reservation is almost unknown outside the confines of the desert southwest. Steve Young would have it no other way.

Jim Dandy is a teacher, counselor, and wrestling coach at the Blanding Middle School, just seven miles from the Navajo Indian Reservation. He is a full-blooded Navajo. Dandy remembers Young's visit to the hogan of Stella Cly just past the highway junction in Monument Valley.

"Steve came there and visited Stella and her family. The people relate to him. He is a great man. He gives them a vision of what a person can do with their lives. He gives hope to our young people and they need hope and encouragement. He is not a man to put on a show. He just gets down and talks as he would to a friend. My son wants to be just like him."

Dandy hears rumors that Young could be close to getting married. He did date a 24-year old woman he met in law school who was shown on national TV sitting by Sherry and Grit at the Super Bowl and accompanying Young during celebrations following the 1994 season. Says Dandy of a possible wedding in Young's future, "If he does, I hope he has his honeymoon down here. He is welcome anytime."

Barbara Schaerrer of Orem, Utah, became one of Young's adopted mothers when Young left home for college as a skinny seventeen-year-old. Outside of Young's immediate family, Schaerrer knows perhaps more about Young's life than anyone; yet she knows almost nothing about Young and the Navajos.

"But he's that way," said Barbara. "Steve is one person who shuns publicity and the spotlight, if you can believe that. He is a great person, very thoughtful of other people and their feelings. I'm anxious to learn what he did with the Navajos because he isn't one to bring it up.

"He is always willing to give of himself," continues Barbara, who joined her husband Doug as Steve Young's special guests at 49er home games throughout the past season. Schaerrer knows what makes Young tick. What people read about and see is the real item. Young is a handsome, articulate, witty, intelligent, gifted athlete; but he is also a wealthy and successful man who is almost embarrassed that he has money. He is not stuck on himself and he is not two-faced.

Wrote Bernie Lincicome of the Chicago Tribune in his post-Super Bowl column: "He has not been a rabid self-promoter as Deion Sanders is or Brian Bosworth was or even the kind of passive participant in fame that Joe Montana has always been. When Young burbled after the game that he and Jerry Rice were going to Disney Acres or where ever it is, I was suddenly aware of how little of this sort of commercial hustling Young had done up until now. This is weird for a

Off the fie_d and onto the green.
Steve Young enjoying one of his favorite pastimes.

two-time league MVP, especially one so glib and at ease with the demands of celebrity."

Young's reply is simple: "I wanted to make my performance speak for itself before I spoke for it."

Barbara Schaerrer has seen it all before. "Steve is very down to earth. He is most comfortable in Levis and a polo shirt. But if he has to, he can wear a tux and look the part of what is expected of him," she says. "Doug helped him buy a used Porsche in Provo. But he was almost ashamed to drive it around town. He took it to California."

Speaking before the World Conference of Mayors, Local Government and Private Sector-Partners on Families on March 19, 1995, in the Tabernacle on Temple Square in Salt Lake City, Young shared what he learned from home. "I believe I would have made a good pioneer. I am 'wired' that way. I can see in myself a work ethic which I believe has come through past generations and has been nurtured by my immediate family and even my football family."

Young told the world leaders that basic principles taught him in his family have never left him. His father taught by example. "Some days I would go to work with him and I noticed he showed the same respect to everyone from the janitor to the president of the company."

The NFL star said he believes God intends for mankind to meet the challenges of a worldwide family, and that recent technological advances in communications that link the world together were put in place for a purpose. "I believe that God is giving us the assignment to meet the ultimate human challenge by creating this sense of family beyond the borders of our homes, cities, states and nations; to include all people of the world, with no thought or prejudice with respect to race, religion or government."

Young said the 49ers had that sense of family. "We are black, white and brown; we are Catholic, Protestant, Mormon, Muslim, Bhuddist and Jewish; we are from every corner of the United States, rich and poor, and we must come together or fall."

His agent, Leigh Steinberg, warned Young his life would change forever as he entered a different level on the world's stage. "Steve's the boy next door—a very bright, enthusiastic boy next door who truly cares about people and does something about it," said Steinberg. "This is a passing. The country's been waiting for this kid. A billion people saw that game. This is the staging event in world sports. People who don't watch football all season watched that game. We have in this country a celebrity-making machine. The whole concept is interesting people, and he's going to be the beneficiary of that."

"You think of the baseball strike, the hockey [lockout], you think of people [like the NBA's Glenn Robinson] saying $72 million is not enough. Now along comes Steve Young, and he's a breath of fresh air, a genuine guy who really cares, a guy who believes in the concept of role models, believes it's imperative."

Steinberg said that Young donated more than $2 million in 1993 to his own Forever Young Foundation for the benefit of underprivileged children in the Bay Area. Young conducts several golf tournaments in California and Utah to raise money for the foundation. A bank is pledging more than $100,000 to be the chief sponsor of the event. Some of the organizations which have tapped into the Forever Young Foundation include Operation Smiles, YMCA of Santa Clara County, Camp Liahona for Deaf Children, Children's Justice Center, ZOHCO, American Sports Institute, Winner on Wheels, Parents of Children with Disabilities, Project Read, Joy of Downs, Literacy Volunteers of America, Spafford Children's Center, Candlelighter's Kids 'N Cancer and Ronald McDonald House.

Steinberg is anxious to sell Young, after all as his agent, he also stands to gain. But Young is an easy sell. Before training camp began following the Super Bowl win over San Diego, Young had signed endorsements worth $3 million and more were on the table.

Steinberg loves Young's attitude. "Steve is a unique person. He's a deep thinker and tremendous competitor who will fight to win every game he can. I don't think politics is out of the question for him sometime in the future. I wouldn't be surprised if ultimately he ends up being a senator from Utah. But he's going to take a long run at this [football]. He's not physically impaired. He's not a real 33," said the agent.

Jim Herrmann, one of Young's best friends and a former BYU teammate was at the NFC championship game with Dallas and at the Super Bowl in Miami. The celebrating Young, seen on televisions all over the world after those two wins, made Herrmann glad Young could finally release. "Steve has never really been able to be himself. Ever. He's always had to hold his feelings inside. It's great to see him be Steve Young again," said Herrmann.

Schaerrer asserts the real Steve Young is a hard worker who refuses to accept defeat. "Even as a freshman playing ball with our kids in the back yard, when he lost, it affected him. He hated to lose." Schaerrer claims that Young does not live an easy life in San Francisco or in Utah. His life is not his own. He has little privacy. There are few simple places he can go, like a grocery store, without people mobbing him. "He has little of a personal life. All these years he's been in San Francisco all alone. He puts a baseball hat on and wears sun glasses to go to the store. There is a price for what he's become, a price few realize."

Steve Young's push to excel in the NFL and finish law school has taken its toll on his personal life. All his best friends have married and have children. Young vowed when he went to Tampa that he'd be married. He almost got married early in his NFL career but plans were cancelled right before the ceremony even though people were flying in from all over the country to attend the wedding. Steve took a long time recovering from that experience, making it hard to open up emotionally to the women he dated. Another burden he packs around is his decision to play football rather than go on a Mormon mission and knock on doors like his father and brothers did. To make up for that lack of service, which he considers extremely important, he has used his position to influence others by taking on speaking engagements and appearance before youth groups nationwide. The Latter-day Saint (Mormon) church headquarters in Salt Lake City knows this and the hierarchy have called him personally with assignments to speak and teach.

Young's personal Achille's heel has been juggling his schedule and dealing with the demands placed upon him—even in his BYU days. Being one who doesn't know how to say no, Young often found himself double-scheduled, blowing off some appointments and rescheduling others Shirley Johnson, the BYU football secretary, has been helping Young since he was a freshman in college. For a few of his 49er years, he even hired Shirley to officially handle his calendar and correspondence. But, luckily for their friendship, that is now being handled by his foundation. "Shirley has been very helpful for Steve," says Schaerrer. "He's used her as a secretary to handle correspondence and has been a loyal friend."

Following the Super Bowl, Leigh Steinberg's secretary started receiving more than 100 letters a day requesting appearances and endorsements by Young. Kaele Porter, director of the Forever Young Foundation, has taken the brunt of the West Coast calls. The foundation will move from San Francisco to Utah this year.

Scott Runia is Young's clergyman, a Mormon bishop in Provo, where Young lives during the off season. Young has spent almost all his adult life speaking at youth devotionals or traveling in the NFL. Even during his college days Young's Sunday schedule was hectic, yet Runia gave Young a church job to do on Sunday when he was not playing football. When in Provo in 1994 Young taught a Sunday School class for children. He was given the five-year old class. There were eight or nine children in his class that summer. Even for the NFL's most elusive quarterback, that is a tough lineup. On his first Sunday teaching, little Grayson Moulton found an open window and crawled outside. Young was paralyzed: He didn't know if he should go get the boy or stay with the rest of the class.

"He got a baptism by fire," said Grayson's mother, Jill Moulton. "The older classes were very jealous. But the kids in this class really didn't know who Steve Young was. They had no concept that he was this great football star. They liked him for who he was, just the teacher. I think that was a good experience for him too." Moulton states that this past year her son and the other kids have learned who their teacher really is and what he does. "When he's played on TV they cheer for him this past season."

One Sunday the Todd and Jill Moulton family came home and heard their son say: "I love Mom, I love Dad. I love my friends. I love Steve. I love popcorn." The Moultons smiled. Their son loved his teacher more than the superstar, a title he does not understand. "It was also good for his dad to know he was listed ahead of Steve," said Jill.

Young is not the only professional athlete who gives time and money to good causes. The league is full of good men who work good causes. Young has agreed time and time again to rework his 49er contract to make room under the salary cap for other teammates. Twice he has rewritten the deal he signed in 1993, and Steinberg says he will do it a third time if it means making the team more competitive. Other NFL stars have done similar things. But Steve Young is the only NFL quarterback who is just following the advice of a famous pioneer statesman, his great-great-great-great grandfather Brigham Young, in doing so. Said Brigham Young of charity: "A man or a woman who places the wealth of this world and the things of time in the scales against the things of God and the wisdom of eternity, has no eyes to see, no ears to hear, no heart to understand."

Steve Young's experience at Disneyland after Super Bowl XXIX helps him keep fame and notoriety in perspective. Jerry Rice joined Young in a one-car parade down Main Street U.S.A. In between the two was Mickey Mouse. They were being driven to a backstage area when they were spotted by two boys, ages six and eight. The six-year old took one look at the trio and jumped towards the car. "It's Mickey Mouse. It's Mickey Mouse!" exclaimed the excited boy. His older brother grabbed him and yanked him back.

"You can't go near Mickey Mouse. Those two big guys will hurt you," said the older sibling.

Comments Steve: "Mickey Mouse is bigger than me and Jerry. I'm doing all right, but I'm not as big as Mickey."

CHAPTER
SEVENTEEN

"We have produced a world of contented bodies and discontented minds."—Adam Clayton Powell

EPILOGUE

The week after Steve Young threw a record six touchdown passes in San Francisco's spanking of the San Diego Chargers in Super Bowl XXIX, Mike Lupica of *Newsday* called Young dull.

Dull? Steve Young?

Lupica, the nationally syndicated sportswriter from New York made the reference in writing about the flashy teammate of Young, the jewelry-laden, superstar Deion "Neon" Sanders. Prime Time Sanders.

Understandable. Sanders and his lightspeed, high-stepping, game-busting, playmaking, endzone dancing persona is all glitter and lights. After the Super Bowl in Joe Robbie Stadium, Sanders appeared before the press in sun glasses in the thick of night, weighed down in multi-carat gold, and draped in an orange suit with no shirt. From the diamonds of Major League Baseball to terrorizing NFL quarterbacks by hogging half the field as a secondary robber, Deion is hot. And it shows.

Steve Young accepting recognition during a
basketball game after his Super Bowl victory.

Epilogue

Wrote Lupica: "Sanders is the one who is going to make the biggest score, in his next contract, in endorsements, even in Hollywood. Young will do all right. He is coming off of one of the most extraordinary seasons a quarterback ever had. But he is as dull to people as he is talented." Continued the writer: "Maybe in another time in sports, Young rightfully would be No. 1 in everybody's hearts. Just not this time."

So, what exactly is this time? And when will be Steve Young's time?

Sports in America are reaching a crescendo as we approach the midnight hour before the dawn of the 21st century. The trouble is, however, that sports are also streaking toward a crest that is anything but dull in ways that are not good.

In the roadkill that is sports in the 90s, America has seen it all in the rearview mirror:

College football and basketball coaches regularly paid more money than university presidents and governors.

Ervin "Magic" Johnson quit playing basketball because the lifestyle he had lived lead to his testing positive for the HIV virus.

Michael Jordan retired from the Chicago Bulls following the death of his father and allegations of mega-dollar gambling because the game wasn't fun any more. Jordan then "un-retired" because he said the young players in the game lacked class and were ruining the game.

A cadre of young NBA players with salaries bigger than the gross national product of many small countries put on a shameful display of spoiled, pouting tantrum-throwing that has league officials and observers worried.

Wrote Phil Taylor in *Sports Illustrated* "A form of insanity is spreading through the NBA like a virus, threatening to infect every team in the league. Alarmingly, its carriers, pouting prima donnas who commit the most outrageous acts of rebellion, include some of the league's younger stars. There is a new outbreak nearly every week, with yet another player skipping practice, refusing his coaches's orders to go into a game, demanding a trade or finding some new and creative way to act unprofessionally. Fines are levied, suspensions imposed, but such measures are nothing in the face of the epidemic. The lunacy is contagious. Madness reigns."

But the NBA didn't make the only headlines. There is the O. J. Simpson trial. And in this twilight before the close of the century, Major League Baseball came to a grinding halt. And it happened right in the middle of one of the most exciting seasons in decades. The players wanted more of the owners' money. And the owners wouldn't give. Both sides were wrong. Both sides were right. But the biggest losers were the fans. When baseball resumed in 1995, fans were very weary of what baseball had put them through.

Wrote *Miami Herald* columnist Edwin Pope: "The players and absolutely the owners, stripped away so much of the cadence and sweetness of our game, including a normal schedule. Into that void rushed a public sense of being defrauded by both sides. Now baseball has to be resold, and only one group can resell it—the players. Or do we know someone who goes to a ball park to watch an owner play?"

And then there was Tonya Harding. It is hard to forget the attack on her chief U.S. figure skating competitor, Nancy Kerrigan. A challenger? Nothing a good clubbing to the knees won't fix.

Epilogue

The courts put former heavyweight boxing champion "Iron" Mike Tyson behind bars for raping a beauty contestant. But after serving half of his six-year prison sentence, Tyson was released just in time to fight for the title and another cache of millions of dollars.

Both Darryl Strawberry and Dwight Gooden, baseball talents for the ages, have wrecked their careers in the prime of life toppled by reckless years of partying, alcohol and cocaine.

"It became a lifestyle for me," Strawberry explained. "Drink, do coke, get women, do something freaky . . . all that stuff. I did it for so long. I played games when I was drunk, or just getting off a drunk or all-night partying or coming down off amphetamines."

America and sports. As the years wear on and the clock ticks down, the money goes up and the expectations mount. A lot of heroes have gone by the wayside and many stars have let their followers down.

Sports have always been a form of escapism. From the gladiators of Rome to the Olympians of Greece, sporting events has sucked civilization into a fantasy world of worshipping the most athletically gifted in our midst.

But it also comes with a price. Stardom is a very heavy weight for athletes to carry.

Said New York Knicks coach Pat Riley of the NBA's egos: "It's running rampant, and it's going to bring down the league one day. It's gotten to where it's all about 'me,' all about recognition, all about contracts, all about playing time, all about lack of rules and discipline."

The time is ripe for America to look at some simple values and how important it is for heroes to embrace those values. Phoenix Suns forward Charles Barkley drew headlines when he told reporters that he was no role model—that nobody in his game should be looked upon or expected to be a role model. Barkley was wrong.

The September 1995 issue of *GQ* magazine devoted its cover to the idea that Steve Young was somehow a cut above what is expected from today's sports heroes. The cover shows Young sporting a white tuxedo, holding a football in one hand and balancing on one foot in the middle of the San Francisco Bay. The headline read: "Steve Young Walks on Water." The article was entitled "The Arm With the Golden Man," by Peter Richmond.

"We've been granted our wish: the consummate good-guy athlete," explains Richmond. "A teetotaling Mormon lawyer, no less. So why aren't we a little more excited about the ascension of Steve Young?"

Richmond addresses the irony of the times by describing how Young has risen to the top of the sports world with his home town values and morals intact, yet is still rarely embraced by a world hungry for good role models.

Richmond continues: "It's not so much that a good man is hard to find. That much we've known for years. It does seem curious, though, that lately, when we find him, we don't seem to want him. We talk a good game, but we've come to prefer decidedly mortal heroes. We've grown so pathological as a species that we can't abide the idea of true heroes among us. Lauding those whose foibles are on a par with our own is much more convenient, and far less taxing on our own self-esteem. How else to interpret our president's favorite poet's singing hosannas at the swearing in of Marion Berry ("A strong man comin' on!") and apologizing profusely for missing Mike Tyson's homecoming rally at the Apollo?"

The *GQ* piece raises an interesting dilemma about what we really want from our super stars. "The truth of it is that we spend most of our waking energy railing about the dearth of propriety in the conduct of our public figures, but when we get what we ask for—when a right-thinking, honest and generous Latter-Day Saint lands in our laps, a complex man who has spent most of his adult life in search of answers, and has found more than a few—about what. exactly, do we want him to enlighten us?" asks Richmond.

"Do we implore him to share the wisdom he gleaned from selling his soul for $40 million to a fly-by-night football league, only to find himself peddling his wares on the bare dirt field of a community college stadium? Do we want to know how in the world he earned a law degree in his off-seasons when, for example, Deion Sanders could boast that, for a period during his tenure at Florida State University, he did not attend any classes at all?"

"No," concludes Richmond. "We want him to tell us how he really feels about Joe Montana—not to get a glimpse of the funky stuff below the sports-page surface but to have Steve Young reveal himself to be as petty and vindictive as the rest of us."

TV talk shows thrive on such revelations. But for nearly two decades of athletic competition, from an All-American quarterback in college to the NFL's Most Valuable Player, Steve Young has cast off disasters and pitfalls that would have tripped up many others. He has shown that it is not just an act. Steve Young is the real thing. What you see is what you get.

If Mike Lupica thinks Steve Young is dull, then maybe we all need less excitement. And perhaps Peter Richmond is right, we may not want it, but the world needs a lesson on how Steve Young has handled the pressures of the pocket: Not in terms of football; but in life.

"Steve Young has proved he is the best quarterback in the NFL," said Neon Deion. But Young is much, much more. He has given the world an example. Perhaps an ideal. He has shown that staying in the pocket takes great patience, trust, and courage. While many of today's "heroes" anxiously scramble out of the pocket to gain a few yards of personal recognition, Steve Young has shown that staying in the pocket of enduring values and principles opens up opportunities to throw for the touchdown pass.